Praise for *TEACHERS DESERVE IT*

For decades, we were told, "Kids first." That sounded like the right thing, yet if we don't take care of teachers first, then who takes care of our students when teachers are run down, exhausted, and overwhelmed? Get ready to fill your bucket as you hear from real educators doing the real work with the right focus, just like you. You have the power to align, and it starts with reading *Teachers Deserve It*!

—**LaVonna Roth**, creator of Ignite Your S.H.I.N.E.®,
ıd chief illuminator

The wisdom, awa  and Adam ignite in
Teachers Deserve n to their local and
state legislators t

—**Traci Browder**, co-founder, GritCrewEDU, author, and host of the podcast Intelligogy

Life takes a village, but the true responsibility of the village is to make sure everyone is getting better daily and pushing the status quo. There's no excuse we can make, because *Teachers Deserve It* has taken away excuses and provides us all with an opportunity!

—**Timothy Alexander**, Emmy Award winner, best-selling author, inspirational speaker, and character coach

Hughart and Welcome provide insights from various perspectives to motivate and inspire educators to remind themselves why education is the best! They challenge us to rekindle our fire and passion for changing lives amid the changing climate around us. With stories embedded throughout the book, they serve to make connections to challenge our thinking and push our mindset. In these trying times, this book fosters the hope we all need to be our best for our students.

—**Neil Gupta, Ed.D.**, district administrator, Ohio

Teachers deserve to be respected and protected! In my more than three decades in education, we have underestimated the value of our teachers, who serve and sacrifice so much for their students. Adam and Rae have given us the blueprint for celebrating and elevating our teachers. They are saving lives each day, so we need to appreciate them! Love them! And honor them! They so deserve It!

—**Salome Thomas-EL, Ed.D.**, award-winning principal, speaker, and author

TEACHERS DESERVE IT

TEACHERS DESERVE IT

WHAT YOU DESERVE.
WHY YOU DON'T HAVE IT.
AND HOW YOU CAN
GO GET IT!

RAE HUGHART AND ADAM WELCOME

Teachers Deserve It: What You Deserve. Why You Don't Have It. And How You Can Go Get It!

© 2020 Rae Hughart and Adam Welcome

This book is available at special discounts when purchased in quantity for educational purposes or as premiums, promotions, or fundraisers. For inquiries and details, contact the publisher at books@daveburgessconsulting.com.

Published by Dave Burgess Consulting, Inc.

San Diego, CA

DaveBurgessConsulting.com

Library of Congress Control Number: 2020941375

Paperback ISBN: 978-1-951600-40-2

Ebook ISBN: 978-1-951600-41-9

Cover and interior design by Liz Schreiter

Editing and production by Reading List Editorial: readinglisteditorial.com

We dedicate this book to all the teachers who show up every single day crushing it for their students, their colleagues, and their school community. Thank you for all that you do. We need you. We appreciate you. We look up to you. We are with you.
Go be awesome, you deserve it!

CONTENTS

INTRODUCTION:

Addressing the Elephant in the Room

Teachers Deserve It started as a discussion over dinner at a table full of educators and turned into a conversation we continued to have with educators around the world. From all these conversations, we learned we have not only a responsibility but an obligation to share the experiences of dedicated educators across the globe.

It's hard to read the news or scroll social media feeds without seeing *something* negative or distasteful about educators, from editorials disparaging teachers going on strike and walking out for higher pay and benefits in record numbers to clueless commenters saying teachers work for the summers off.

In school systems all over the country, teachers are demanding better pay, better benefits, smaller class sizes, counselors, librarians, support teachers—the list goes on and on. It's easy for many Americans, within and outside of education, to recognize that our teachers need more. But it goes beyond need.

We're here to tell you that teachers *deserve* more.

ADAM SAYS

In the Bay Area, where I live, a teacher's salary is well below the poverty line, and some districts simply can't recruit teachers because they can't afford to live in the same town where they teach. In San Francisco, for instance, the average teacher's annual salary is $55,000, and the poverty line is around $59,000. Those numbers together just don't work.

When I was a principal, many of the teachers on my staff were "super commuters" who drove 90–120 minutes each way or lived like college students, with multiple roommates just to make ends meet.

RAE SAYS

When I originally began teaching, I had very little understanding of what I was getting myself into. I had no idea what a teacher deserved because what teachers deserved was rarely discussed. In my mind, teachers had it easy. Come on . . . they don't even work over the summer, right?

Nevertheless, within the first six months of having the title of "teacher," I was coping with immense stress, counseling students who were taken from their homes, and planning personalized lessons each day to meet the needs of my diverse learners, and I'd been subpoenaed to speak on a student's behalf—all while living on a nearly unlivable wage.

From our own experiences and in talking to colleagues, it has become clear that teachers are not getting what they deserve and something has to be done.

Don't get us wrong: it's not just about the money. Teachers deserve much more than a larger paycheck each month.

Teachers deserve respect. Teachers deserve time. Teachers deserve strong leadership.

Teachers deserve a whole lot.

This is not a book that demands that those who are ignorant of the struggles in education learn about the hardships of teachers. Nor is it a book focused on placing blame for the lack of change in the educational system over the last century.

This book is a call to arms for a movement.

This book asks teachers to take a stand for what we deserve and begin the process of controlling the narrative. Teachers must learn to share their stories out in the public sphere and must seek out other educators in their networks doing the same. It is more important than ever for teachers to project their voices so we can have lasting change.

This book is for leaders. No matter your leadership position, you should be ready to advocate for teachers and build them up, and never forget what it's like to be in the classroom full time. Do all that is humanly possible to listen, support, and advocate for your teachers. Stand behind them, next to them, or in front of them—that's what is needed right now.

This book is for teachers. Complaining is not a strategy and will only get us further away from what we deserve and what we need in order to successfully support the students we work with. Having a solution-oriented mindset is positive, it's proactive, and it's what will lead to the greatest change.

Therefore, this book is filled with easy-to-implement ideas for teachers, leaders, and anyone working with students. At the end of every chapter, we have included a #TeachersDeserveIt Educator Experiment that will push your thinking in new ways to broaden your perspective as an educator.

This book is also an attempt to humanize the teachers who are waking up every day and giving their very best for the students they work with. We're putting names to faces and their "whys" to the profession. We want you to see that teachers are human, they're parents, they're voters, they're sons and daughters of teachers, and they often have a long lineage of educators in their family. They're real and they deserve respect, because what they do is the most important job on the planet.

You cannot change people, but you can influence them to choose change. Why?

Because teachers deserve it.

CHAPTER ONE
Teachers Deserve Appreciation and Respect

Teachers can get a bad rap; we've seen it for years. A lack of respect and appreciation has permeated our culture for far too long.

You're a teacher because you want summers off?

You're a teacher so you can be home at 3:00 p.m. every day?

You're a teacher because you couldn't do anything else?

Wrong!

You're a teacher because you care about kids. And you know how to build relationships with them in order to help those children maximize their full potential socially and academically. Teachers so often put their own needs before their students, because that's what teachers do.

RAE SAYS

Have you ever taken a personality test and disliked the results? Recently the Enneagram personality test has been a focal point of my friends' conversations. While I continue to be skeptical of the test itself, my friends keep bringing up my Enneagram score when we hang out and in texts. I just can't seem to escape it, and I didn't like my score.

Why? People with my Enneagram type tend to be ambitious, focused, and serious in their behavior. They are very career-oriented and are more introverted than other types. They tend to find much of their identity in their work and seek affirmation from those around them.

I have continued to struggle with this assessment for multiple reasons. However, I think the majority of my discomfort stems from the social construct of what a teacher should be. I feel as though teachers who have these traits are often perceived negatively because of them.

The truth is, I'm still uncomfortable with the results of my Enneagram test in part because I find it shameful to be unsatisfied with my hard work without the affirmation of others. Needing others' approval seems juvenile, and I worry it might make others think that the intention behind what I do is rooted in a self-serving space. But that is not my truth.

I want to feel proud of my work, and I want to enjoy every moment of being a qualified professional. And more than anything else, I want to feel trusted by my families as someone who's wonderfully qualified to serve their children.

Childhood stories and society have painted a picture of what a classroom teacher looks like. They are seen as simple, generous, and quixotic personalities who would never dare ask for recognition of their work. They aren't real people. They live in their classrooms. Teachers don't have lives outside of their job. They don't need anything for themselves. Teachers are obedient. Teachers go into the profession in order to have summers off. Teachers are people who could not make it in the corporate mainstream.

But we know better.

Teachers are strong.

Teachers are selfless.

Teachers are creative.

Teachers are educated.

Teachers are innovative and full of new and relevant ideas.

Teachers are voters.

Teachers are jugglers.

Teachers are problem solvers.

Teachers are soldiers.

Teachers show up every day to support, encourage, care for, and educate our children.

Teachers deserve to be admired and appreciated.

Politicians, entrepreneurs, and professional athletes often have characteristics similar to educators. Typically, people in these professions have bold, daring personalities. These careers often attract problem solvers and change makers. And with these characteristics, we see these individuals continually appreciated for their dedication, passion, outspokenness, and hard work.

Yet when teachers exhibit the same traits, they are considered overbearing and out of place, and are continuously silenced by society.

Have you seen that comic floating around that compares a parent-teacher conference in 1969 to one in 2011? In the 1969 panel, the parents are holding up a report card asking the child to explain his grades. In the 2011 panel, the same family has shifted their focus from the student to the teacher, who's now the one being interrogated about the bad grades. The teacher, sitting behind a desk, is illustrated as nervous, shy, and guilty.

Is that the kind of educator we want to be teaching the future leaders of our communities? Someone who whimpers behind their desk and is the first person to act guilty when questions arise?

Let's put it this way: When your car needs to be repaired, would you leave it with a mechanic you had a sneaking suspicion you should not trust? If red flag after red flag came up, would you still hand the mechanic your keys? Wouldn't you prefer a credible professional? Someone who was knowledgeable about cars and whose walls were plastered with awards and thank-you cards from previous customers? Would you view such a display as boastful? Or does this sense of "bragging" feel different because you are leaving a valuable possession in the hands of a trusted worker?

Children are the most prized members of our community. And yet, as a society, we seem to be uncomfortable with the idea of appreciating and trusting the successful professionals we've entrusted our children to.

Teachers deserve to be appreciated for their strengths.

RAE SAYS

I have been fortunate enough to work for a number of different principals in my career. Each educational leader has challenged my thinking and allowed me to have the flexibility to do most of what I want to do to best serve my students. However, there was one principal who not only challenged me as an educator in the classroom but as a human being as well.

Christopher McGraw and I met for coffee recently. Chris has been my principal for some time, and I am confident in saying he's made more of an effort to get to know me as a person than any other leader I have worked with in the past.

He is a relationship guy. He wants to learn about his teachers as the incredible educators they are, and he also aims to learn their stories—similar to how we, as teachers, aim to learn the stories of our students.

Over coffee, we discussed the Enneagram test. I griped about the way the explanation made me feel like a selfish person—aiming to please others for the sake of my own success rather than aiming simply to serve those around me. Was that really my "why" in education? Accolades and fame?

Because if this was the case, I was in the wrong business.

After I concluded my rant, he asked me a very simple question: "How does someone else help to fill your bucket?"

Have you heard this metaphor before? It is a common analogy to describe the need to take care of yourself, so you can best care for those around you.

It's the same message they share on airplanes before take-off: "Put on your mask before assisting others."

Striving to be insightful, I told Chris the best way I fill my bucket is by spending purposeful time with my family. Even just thirty minutes can shift my mood for the better!

He nodded and then asked the question for a second time—this time with more emphasis on the words *someone else*: "How can someone else help to fill your bucket?"

"A lot of ways!" I responded, listing off a few different examples I think every teacher enjoys (e.g., morning donuts, a little note, a surprise coffee, etc.).

"Okay." He paused. "But what fills your bucket up the fastest?"

After a long pause, I responded, "Someone seeing me." I explained, "I work my butt off each day, and when someone takes a moment to notice, it fills me right back up."

"That's your superpower," he responded.

The act of being self-aware enough to know the best way for others to help you is a superpower only the most effective teachers possess. You can use this power to your advantage, to propel you forward. If you know the most valuable way to be successful, why wouldn't you use that superpower as often as possible?

What's to be embarrassed about? Wouldn't you prefer to know how to fill another person's bucket in the most efficient and effective way possible, rather than purchasing a dozen donuts and having a smaller impact?

Every teacher has a different way in which they feel appreciated, and taking a moment to identify what this is for you can supercharge the way others support you.

Remember: there's no "wrong way" to feel valued or seen. Wanting appreciation from others is a natural desire teachers deserve to express.

ADAM SAYS

As a principal, it was my responsibility to know what was going on in my building. I loved getting into classrooms and exploring with students as they began to learn something new.

And let me tell you, if you want to make teachers feel absolutely amazing, share your appreciation with them! My favorite way to show my appreciation was to bring a teacher their favorite coffee drink and leave a handwritten note on their desk in the morning. You might be wondering, "How did you know their favorite coffee drink, Adam?"

I asked each of them at the beginning of the year and kept a note on my phone. If someone had done something amazing the day before, they got a coffee and a note. If a teacher was going through a difficult time in their personal life or dealing with a challenging parent, they got a coffee and a note.

Bringing coffee and handwriting a note is simple. But it shows that you care. It shows that you took the time to write the note and learn what their favorite coffee was. It shows that you're in tune with what's happening in their life. It shows that you know how much celebrating teachers do for other teachers, and it reminds them that they matter to you and the larger school organization.

There are hundreds of ways you can show your appreciation for teachers at a community level. Whether it be with a celebratory note in an all-staff email or a handwritten message to a teacher that you leave in their mailbox or getting on the intercom and celebrating that teacher in front of the entire school, show others they are seen. Here are some of our other favorite ways to appreciate teachers!

- Bring them a snack you know they just love, or have a traveling basket with different options.
- If you're the principal, cover their class the last hour one day and send them home early. Everyone would love some more time in the day, so do that for your teachers.
- If you're a parent, don't send a teacher an email in the evening that they may worry about or that will keep them up at night. Wait until the next morning.
- Brag about them on social media. Take a picture of them or the two of you together, and say something awesome!
- Offer to write a Donors Choose grant for them. Writing the grant can be super time-consuming, and who doesn't love free stuff for their classroom?
- Tell them face to face how much you care about them. Words matter and people remember how you talk to them, especially the kind words!

TAKING IT INTO OUR OWN HANDS

Yes, all of these ideas are awesome, but as educators, we cannot wait for others to show us the appreciation we need to do our best. Consider a similar situation: You have a middle school student who has realized they need support on a math concept. Following this moment of need, the student slouches down in their seat with their hand raised just above the top of their head.

A few minutes later, you notice the student. You had been conferencing with a small group of students at the front of the room and told students to problem-solve during the three-minute conference. What do you do?

An important element of learning is learning how to learn. Teaching a student how to be an advocate for their needs as a learner allows students to act as reflective, active participants in the learning process.

RAE SAYS

In my sixth-grade classroom, we talk a great deal about the need for students to take ownership over their learning. While using a mastery learning framework, students have the opportunity to receive a personalized learning-focused education—getting students what they need when they need it.

However, this system does not come without its hurdles. In most cases, students have little experience taking ownership (or the opportunity to take ownership) over their learning journey prior to my class. Therefore, conversation after conversation focuses on the need for students to take life by the reins and to not allow anyone to hold them back!

Last week, a group of community members joined our classroom. Their intention was to connect their experience in their professional careers with the math content students were learning. Students were instructed to move throughout their learning as usual while partnering with the community members. Students were asked to show our guests the ropes and walk them through their learning while talking about how this math was relevant in their adult lives.

Beth, a guest in my classroom for the first hour, came up to me after the first class wide-eyed. "This was the most interesting class I had ever been in," she celebrated.

Now let's have some teacher talk right here: Beth was partnered with a very challenging student. Therefore, when Beth shared her comment with me, my initial thought was, *Oh gosh, what did Maggie do now?*

Beth gave me the play by play: "I was working with her on decimals when we came across a multiplication problem she didn't understand. Suddenly she stood up and said, 'Come with me, we need to collaborate with a few people in the room to figure this out.'

"So, I stood up and followed her to the front of the room.

"'This is our tracking page,' Maggie explained. 'See these blue markers? That means they are currently working on this section of their learning. We want to find green markers. That means they are masters at the content.'

"We chose a green marker from the list and walked over to the student group.

"'Can you help me with this?' Maggie asked.

"'For sure!' the student exclaimed, pausing the video she was recording."

Beth continued, expanding on the student's leadership.

My favorite part of the story?

What Beth shared had happened after the student understood the content.

Following the students' interaction, they returned to their original seats. Here, Beth asked Maggie, "Why didn't you just raise your hand?"

The student's response was perfect.

Confused, Maggie responded, "Why would I do that? No one can stop my learning except me. If I raised my hand and sat quietly, I would have made a choice to stop my learning. Is that what you do at work when something is challenging? You just sit and wait for someone to fix it?"

Now I know I am someone who greatly appreciates being affirmed by others—but if I sat around and waited for it to happen, I'd be waiting a long time!

Why would you, as a teacher, put that much control in someone else's hands?

Other people are busy, other people are preoccupied, and most people don't know what is going on in your classroom. If you want to be appreciated by others, you first need to turn the tables and start celebrating others. Lead by example.

Students love being appreciated. Gold stars, smiley face stickers, a *Good Job* written at the top of their paper, and end-of-the-year certificates make students smile. Think back to your favorite memory of your youth. Our bet is that it was a special occasion when you were shown appreciation in some way—maybe a youth ballet recital or school play.

No one can appreciate what you're doing for your students if they don't know what you're doing in your classroom. Share it! Begin by sharing it with your colleagues or administrator.

"Hey! I did something awesome today in class and the students loved it!"

"Gosh, I took a risk today. Can I tell you about it?"

In the twenty-first century, when social media became a major topic of discussion, most of us created our own accounts, chose a flattering profile picture, and hopped on the bandwagon. Who did you follow first? Well, the people you knew and names you recognized. For many, this included the president, their best friend, and Kim Kardashian, right?

You might have heard the phrase "every solution to the problems in our classrooms exists in a classroom somewhere in the world. We just need to find it." Well, it's time to find those solutions for others, friends!

If your social media feeds are filled with self-promoting educators, you are following the wrong people. Social media is not about bragging on your classroom success, but sharing in the goings-on in the classroom.

Share your reflections, your hurdles, adventures, successes, and resources. It's not about you—it's about supporting the educators connected with you in the interest of better-quality work. By doing so, you are building your own PLN (professional learning network) and contributing to the field of education. And then, when your feed changes to educators dedicated to being a part of a virtual community of growth-minded teachers, share your appreciation with them!

The question is, why are you waiting for someone else to begin making this shift?

You have the power to begin this movement.

RAE SAYS

One of my favorite things to do on Instagram is send a message to an educator I am connected to and show my appreciation for something awesome they are doing.

It takes fifteen seconds.

I simply head to their profile, click the Message button, and record a quick fifteen-second personalized message to them.

Here's an example: "Hey, Kelsey! I just wanted to say thank you for all that you are doing with students! Your post last week about beginning to code with your first graders was awesome! I love that you chose to step outside of the box and take on a new challenge. I see you, girl! Keep it up!"

TEACHERS ALSO DESERVE RESPECT

Teachers spend their days being continually questioned. They are interrogated about their lesson plan structure and how they handled a student's behavior. They are asked why they work such long hours. Frankly, it's unusual for a teacher to go a single day without a spouse, administrator, or colleague questioning their intentions.

Can you volunteer for this student event?

Who did you communicate that to?

What are you going to do to increase those test scores?

Where is that form I asked you to fill out?

When will you have that finished?

Why is this student unsuccessful?

How are you communicating that change with your families?

Why haven't you implemented the new character education program?

The new Chromebooks are still in the cart. Why haven't they been implemented into your lessons?

The who, what, where, why, and how happening outside of the classroom instruction is exhausting. It's disrespectful. We're sick and tired of the questions, so let's ask our own.

Why am I not trusted in my building?

What time can I take for my family without feeling shame?

Why am I not paid more for the important work I do?

Where can I find professional development that will encourage me to grow?

When will I finally get the support my kids deserve?

Why can't I make all the copies I need without having to count every single one and not go over my monthly allocation?

Why am I not respected?

Why do some parents think it's my fault if their child isn't on grade level?

Why do some leaders think it's my fault if some of my students aren't proficient?

The way teachers are treated as they do their work is disrespectful, and it needs to change.

ADAM SAYS

I got to my first school as a principal, and not one single teacher had a classroom website. It just wasn't something that had been part of the culture before I arrived.

Now twenty years ago teachers having a website wasn't a thing, but in today's world it's not only a great way to communicate with families but also helps explain who you are and your "why."

As a principal I rarely ever made a sweeping directive with staff, but this was one that had to happen, and there were reasons behind the decisions. When initially meeting with teachers that summer when I took over, one complaint they had was the amount of emails from parents asking about dates, information, forms to fill out, etc.

Fast-forward a few months once everyone had a classroom website, I asked at a staff meeting, "Has the number of emails from parents gone down? Do you feel parents are better informed about what's happening in your classroom?"

There was silence for a few minutes, and then hands started going up. Across the board, emails had gone way down, and teachers felt better understood by parents and were overall happier with their classrooms.

Now of course creating a website isn't the magic formula, but if you want the community to understand you, putting out information about your classroom and yourself is paramount.

BE THE CHAMPION

One of the most viewed educational TED Talks in the world was delivered in 2013 by Rita Pierson. Pierson, a longtime educator, titled her twenty-minute talk "Every Kid Needs a Champion." One line from her talk in particular continues to echo across teaching circles: "Kids don't learn from people they don't like."

Brittany Dixon

Fifth-Grade Teacher
North Carolina

FUN! A simple, three-letter word that has a long-lasting impact on students. I teach because I believe that through positive and productive relationships, academic rigor, and a touch of the unexpected, all children can develop into curious, creative, lifelong learners. I open the doors to learning through engagement and by inspiring my students to explore their own curiosities.

Teaching brings me great joy, and I strive to instill a love for learning in my students. Through singing, dancing, and celebrating each other's victories, my students attain higher levels of learning. They are pushed beyond their limits, all while having fun. I believe in endless possibilities for my students because someone believed in me.

The idea of building relationships with students is an ever-evolving conversation between educators. Twitter chats, blogs, YouTube videos, Instagram stories, and Teachers Pay Teachers resources have been flooded with tools for educators to implement purposeful learning opportunities to get to know students.

Need an activity for a middle school advisory lesson? Download a free guide to support the facilitation of a restorative circle. Looking to collect a little data on your students' thoughts or opinions? Create a quick student inventory survey and administer it during the first few weeks of school.

Relationships. Relationships. Relationships.

But what if we rewrote Pierson's tagline to encompass an unsupported area in the educational mainstream?: "People don't respect people they don't understand."

People—parents, administration, community members, and even students—cannot choose to be allies and give respect to those they don't know.

We see this reaction across all professions.

ADAM SAYS

One of the very first things I did as a new principal was meet with every teacher and classified staff member at my new school. The email I sent before we met had a few simple questions for everyone to think about prior to our meeting.

What makes you proud to work at this school?

What's something you'd like me to know about this school?

What do you feel is your biggest strength as an educator?

Those humble beginnings established a framework of trust and respect with my new staff. Meetings should not be about the leader talking the entire time; they should be about everyone sharing and connecting and becoming a stronger educational team.

One moment that really stands out was when a teacher called me in the evening only a few months into the school year. Something had happened with a parent who was upset with them, and they were worried about the situation and wanted to let me know what was going on and ask for advice.

Ten years later, I don't even remember all the details of the situation, but it also doesn't matter. The teacher needed support. They needed their administrator to listen, ask questions, support them, and continue to build a relationship with the student and family in question, so that the teacher could get the needed respect they deserved. What I told them was, essentially, "We're going to deal with this situation together, and it's going to be okay."

What Adam was doing in his meetings with teachers was giving them a chance to tell him about their "why." We all could have chosen a hundred different professions, but teaching is different. You know it, and we know it—we choose to teach because we choose to make a difference. The WHY. This is the easiest way for a teacher to be better understood (and thus better respected) by parents and the community. Why did you become a teacher? And once you've articulated that, it's important for your leadership to support you.

QUESTIONS TO HELP YOU EXPLAIN YOUR WHY:

- Why do you wake up so early?
- Why do you spend 180 days a year with other people's children rather than your own?
- Why do you fight tooth and nail to find tools, facilitate interventions, and incorporate student voices?
- Why do you take hours to write grants to fund the unfunded?
- Why do you work weekends?
- Why don't you take personal days?
- Why do you attend conferences over the summer while you are off of work?

EXPLAINING YOUR WHY

Teachers deserve the opportunity to explain their reasons for becoming educators. The better colleagues, students, parents, and administration understand an educator's drive to be in the classroom and work with students throughout the school year, the more capable we'll be of earning respect for this selfless profession. It's almost like a public relations department for a company.

Think of your "why" as your statement that says to the world, "This is who I am and why I teach." Every educator's approach toward education is rooted in different experiences they had during their upbringing. For some, the "why" in becoming an educator is rooted in a relationship with a teacher who inspired them to see success within themselves. For others, it stems from a distasteful learning experience that sparked a need for change.

RAE SAYS

Learning was always an uphill battle for me. I felt like I was wearing Rollerblades.

Two steps forward. One big roll back.

Catch yourself with your hands. Stand back up. And try again.

Two steps forward. One big roll back.

After being diagnosed with SLD in reading and writing, I was provided all the support my Chicagoland school system and dedicated family could offer. Small class sizes, modified material, and tutoring sessions three times a week became a never-ending tap dance.

Every day was a continual reminder of my shortcomings.

I think I am the only sixth-grade math teacher in the history of the world who earned a D in sixth-grade math. Ironic, huh? Nothing in school made sense, and the only saving grace I had was when I came across an educator committed to more than test scores, who was interested in building relationships.

Within my career-driven family, setting goals for the future was a constant topic of dinnertime conversation. The evening I announced I wanted to become an educator, my sister about choked.

"You hate school!"

Yeah, I did. But I had a "why" to change it.

Rae's history helps explain her why. Teachers telling these kinds of stories is part of how our communities will open their eyes and give teachers the respect they deserve.

It's time to speak up and share your "why"! If not now, when?

THE BEGINNING

Teachers prepare for hours to welcome in the new school year. You can tell it's finally August when the memes of teachers eagerly awaiting the go-ahead from custodial staff to enter the building to begin the new school year flood social networking platforms.

RAE SAYS

For those of you who know me, you know memes are essentially my love language. So, I have to give a shout-out to the *Friends* meme of four members of the cast sticking their heads through the locked door looking into the apartment.

The image is often captioned "Teachers waiting to get into their classrooms."

If you haven't seen this one, pause here and search on Google. It's worth a good laugh . . . because hey, teachers deserve a good laugh as well!

The beginning of the year is a perfect time to start your "why" communication. Whether you participate in an open house event, send a newsletter, use a website, or communicate through a tech tool, make your communication with families focused on your "why" over the procedural information. This does not mean you shouldn't share the tidbits of your classroom to your team—we are all about sharing details with your stakeholders—but allow the conversation to be framed with the "why" as the focal point of the course requirements.

It's not only about what we do in our classrooms but how we bring others in to understand the "why" behind our practice as soon as they join our classroom family. As educators, we are filled with a natural desire to bring learning to life for our students by helping them find the "why" behind what they're learning.

What if we had that same requirement for teachers? Can you imagine the purposefulness you would find in focusing less on the procedural elements of your classroom and more on the "why" behind your methodologies? Talk about the first step toward being understood and earning the respect you deserve.

RAE SAYS

Following my time in school, I was handed a diploma and told to go change the world! As a foolish, passion-driven teacher, my answer was, "Yup! No worries! I'll make that happen!"

Nevertheless, the reality set in when I realized education was full of puzzle pieces.

Some of the puzzle pieces focused on instructional best practices. Some of the puzzle pieces dealt with student engagement. Others had to do with the politics that come along with the educational profession. But how do you put them together to make a fully rendered picture?

Out of sheer necessity, I designed what later became the Teach Further model—a unit design framework focusing on the "why" behind content through the use of student-themed internships sponsored by local businesses.

Here, I was able to finally take all of the educational puzzle pieces, like student goal setting, relevancy, problem solving, and personalized learning, and implement them with fidelity.

But the trick was not only finding the glue that would hold all of these best practices together but dedicating some serious time to explaining it to my families early on in the school year.

BECOME AN ACTIVE MEMBER OF YOUR COMMUNITY

People don't respect people they do not understand.

The first step toward developing an understanding for someone is to spend time with them and have a hundred conversations about nothing.

RAE SAYS

I had a tough school year in 2019. It seemed as though each day was set up for success, and yet I kept getting derailed forty-five minutes into the school day. As a sixth-grade teacher, I felt as though I had seen it all:

Struggling learners. Check.

District-mandated initiatives. Check.

Tough co-workers. Check.

Trauma-affected students. Check.

Piles of paperwork. Check.

Uninformed parents. Check.

The list goes on and on.

But a student in my first hour was a mystery to me. One moment Parker was having an outburst brought on by rage. Five minutes later, he was a little boy, full of jokes and comic-book-driven stories.

Each day was a rollercoaster, and I was never sure if Parker would be full of bellyaching jokes or painful pitfalls. I had two options: provide

Parker with disciplinary action after disciplinary action, or get to the root of the problem and learn his story.

The best decision I ever made was asking if Parker would have lunch with me. Sitting over school cafeteria chicken fingers and mashed potatoes, we chatted. One lunch turned into two, and suddenly we found time to have lunch together two times a week.

Sometimes we talked about video games. Other times we discussed school conflicts and strategically problem-solved his frustrations. It was during these lunch opportunities that I finally learned Parker's story.

Living in a single-parent household, Parker's father worked third shift at a business in town. His mother had passed just a year prior from a drug overdose. And his favorite memories were spending time with Grandma, who lived about two and a half hours from his home.

I'd had no idea what Parker was dealing with outside of my forty-six-minute math class.

I am so honored he shared his story with me.

People cannot effectively support people they do not know—but everyone has a story. Knowing those stories helps us know how to better support people. So, if you as a teacher need to be better respected, you've got to get out there and share your story. How are you choosing to share your story? Who are you choosing to share your story with?

The truth is, we cannot blame others for not seeing our viewpoints if we do not choose to articulate our "why." So, it's time to change!

Be vulnerable. Be daring. Let someone see you.

RAE SAYS

I have been an active member within my community for a few years. I sit on community boards, take leadership roles in religious affiliations, support small businesses, and we network—a lot.

In doing this, I have not only made stronger connections with others doing purposeful work but have allowed for conversations around education to grow organically. These conversations have led to families better understanding choices made by the district and shed light on concerning areas of our school system.

Honestly, the best conversation was one I had seven years ago with the owner of a local pizza company, who later helped me design a full unit around the relevancy of math in his small business. He now donates hundreds of pizzas to my students each year, visits to mentor students during their math internship, and hosts a community night celebrating students' math skills each year.

Boy, did that quick conversation grow into a lifelong partnership—between myself and the owner, of course—but it also created an opportunity for our community to invest in the success of our student body.

He understood and connected with my "why."

Begin by joining a local group within your community. Do you love art? There's probably an art club at your YMCA or neighborhood gallery. Enjoy interior design? Join a social media group to talk shop. Believe in a cause? A local organization probably needs a dedicated volunteer.

The more others get to know you and understand your passions, your growth areas, and your success stories, the more our stakeholders, community leaders, and colleagues can make decisions with our best interest in mind.

But if you don't let anyone learn your story, the only one to blame is yourself.

COMMUNICATE DIFFERENTLY

Digital communication has disrupted the way people communicate in the professional world. In the late 1800s, a postman would visit a business every month with a sack of letters. But let's be honest, by the time a message arrived, it was already three weeks old.

Now, back then, that was as up-to-date as you could be. Only those wealthy enough may have had the option of picking up the phone. While transportation methods continued to evolve, the largest shift in communication came with the invention of email and the digital age we live in now.

We no longer need to operate in a micro-community, where our only contacts include those we are personally connected to. Today, you can forge connections with people around the world simply by hopping on to your preferred social networking platform and clicking two buttons.

Picture an accounting department in the 1900s. It was a large space filled with rows of desks where employees were doing arithmetic—problem after problem. Today, this entire room of mathematicians can be replaced with a single computer using a single function in a Google Sheet.

The factory-based industrialized model revolutionized education, and classrooms were constructed to reflect this atmosphere. Yet, this industrialized model is no longer current and doesn't reflect the world students walk into when they walk out of your classroom.

The digital age didn't arrive without a great deal of fear—we continue to hear echoes of these anxieties today:

"Kids these days live on their phone."

"This generation has no social skills!"

"Kids only communicate through their phones."

How do we restore a bit of "human nature" into the digital communication world? How do we share our "why" in a way that resonates with how our students, parents, and colleagues communicate now?

RAE SAYS

I vividly remember being on a live video with my friend Tiffany Ott when she unintentionally changed the way I communicated with families forever. We were on a Facebook Live conversation discussing classroom strategies when we arrived on the topic of parent communication.

Oh, did I get on my soapbox!

"I hate email!" I rambled. "It completely takes away what I love about communication and leaves all the bad components—spelling and assumed tone. Yuck!"

Then Tiffany shared the best idea with me: "Have you ever considered doing a video email?"

We get it, no one enjoys being on camera. Even in the days of Snapchat and Instagram, where people around the world showcase photos of themselves, being on camera might seem like a great deal of work.

But consider the reality of video in our progressive day and age. If you chose to share the same content you'd normally put into a newsletter in a video format, you reclaim the power to control the narrative. Via video, your viewers can hear your tone and witness your expressions, and they typically retain more information from you than from a six-paragraph email text.

Imagine a world where you didn't need to "convince" someone of your feelings by finding the perfectly crafted sentence, stifled by the limitation of tone within your writing. Instead, share your passion with your audience the way you know best—by being and acting like you!

The scale in which we interact with the world has changed. The micro-society now operates on a global scale. It's time to connect and communicate with your audience in a way that they can best benefit from.

So, the next time you have a quick update for your stakeholders, flip on your camera.

Allow your network to learn about you. Allow your network to witness your passion. Allow your network to see you. Allow your network to see why you deserve their respect.

Choose to communicate differently.

Ciji Thurman

Third-Grade Teacher
Kentucky

I come to school daily not because of the money or because it is just a job, but because I love what I do. More importantly, I love the students that I get the honor to teach and guide every day. I have always enjoyed school. I chose to be a teacher after doing some volunteering in a nearby elementary school. At the time, my niece was in elementary school, and I decided to help out in the classroom. It was during that time I felt like not only was teaching something I could do, but it was something I WANTED to do and knew I could be successful in.

With my mother also being in education for many years, I knew that I would have the support I would need to start and continue my journey in education. Teaching, in my opinion, is truly a calling. My goal is to touch the life of at least one child, to make a difference in at least one life. This is my "why."

I want to open my world to students. I don't want to just teach them the academics that are necessary in life; I also want to reach a student on a much deeper level. Each day I come to school knowing it will be a fresh start. I know that each day is going to hand me something different.

Each week we do a Wednesday morning meeting. During that time, the students get the chance to share aloud and talk as a class in a "safe space." It is at that time I get many of my ideas on the "how" to teach content. We as educators, no matter the level, have standards to go by, but those standards tell us what to teach, not how to teach it. I use this time to get to know my scholars and allow them to get to know each other, and I use the information I collect to guide how to better reach them academically. When I change my room into a hospital, restaurant, or even a Monopoly game, it is because I have gained information from my students. Each day, our students are telling us how to reach them, and it is up to us to listen.

I believe that success comes not from the career you decide to pursue, or the money you make, but from your character. I am inspired so often by so many different educators and even the scholars in our room. I don't think anyone has a single mentor; we're mentored by so many without even knowing it. I find that the people that really inspire me to be great are those scholars I stand in front of daily. They push me to be great. We can't expect something from our students that we don't expect from ourselves. The children today are our future, and I want to be able to show the students that walk into my classroom that they are loved, welcomed, and capable of great things.

A few years back, I had a student that was having a hard time at home, and that would translate into her schoolwork at times. I could not blame her, nor did I shame her for this. I empathized with her and made sure that she knew that I was there if she needed me, and that I would never leave her. I did not know it at the time, but just our small conversations, our lunch dates, and our encouraging letters really made a difference in her world. She ended up moving to a different state; I had no way to contact her after the first month of her leaving.

Just recently, this student contacted me via email. She is currently in high school and wanted to share with me that she has never forgotten about me or the things I said to her. She wrote, "I will get through this and you give me that confidence. Ever since I moved, there hasn't really been a day that I haven't thought about you. You made a huge impact on me and my sight of life." Those words meant more to me than anything. Knowing that you have put a stamp on the heart of another makes all the not-so-good days worth it. In this profession, you may not always see instant results, but then, as they say, "The day you plant the seed is not the day you eat the fruit." In short, my "why" is to empower students to use their voice and their special gifts to make this world a better place.

MAKING IT STICK

Just like our students, we must do a formative assessment of our audience. Formative assessment is used continually in classes to evaluate student understanding. The goal is to evaluate mastery and use the data to drive future instruction. This same strategy must be used on our audience as we work to explain our "why" to earn the trust and respect of our communities.

Do your administrators and parents know your "why" yet? Do you need to do some re-teaching? An easy way to assess understanding is simply to ask. At your next parent-teacher conference or back-to-school night, provide families with a survey. As one of your survey questions, ask families about their understanding of your "why". If you sense it hasn't stuck yet, it's time to get to work.

Your "why" must be articulated in the same way you'd introduce any new concept in the classroom:

- Pre-test
- Communicate the information
- Allow time for questions
- Remind, re-teach, review
- Repeat

Teaching can become routine. Daily lesson plans, meetings, emails, grading, and other tools can help you get into the flow of a school year but can also put you on autopilot. Getting really clear on your "why" and making sure everyone you interact with knows what it is, is the best way to stay purpose-driven in your teaching and to show up for yourself, your students, and your colleagues with respect and appreciation.

We are for teachers. We support teachers. Let's change the narrative around respect. Let's share our why.

#TEACHERSDESERVEIT
EDUCATOR EXPERIMENT

1. Choose to share your appreciation for another teacher today! Send out a tweet, pick up an extra Starbucks order, or simply write a kind handwritten note. Take it a step further and call another teacher you know on social media that lives in another state. Find out where they work, call the school, and tell them you admire the work they do. That gesture really goes a long way! Model the good you hope to see in the world by celebrating a teacher! Why? Because teachers deserve to be appreciated!

2. It's time to introduce yourself! Create a thirty-second video addressed to the stakeholders in your community. You can do this on your phone or laptop. No editing needed! Post your video on your favorite social media platform or send it directly to your viewers via email. It does not need to be fancy—simply put yourself out there and share your "why." Ready for one step further? Share your video using #TeachersDeserveIt for others to see!

CHAPTER TWO

Teachers Deserve to Be Heard

Teachers deserve to have a voice across all aspects of a school. Teachers deserve to make the call more often at their schools when it comes to programs, initiatives, and being a part of the team. Teachers deserve to use their voices to question the rules more often, because if we're not questioning the rules, we're doing ourselves and our students a disservice. And teachers deserve to bring their voices together to use a united front, to be heard in all matters that affect them, period.

TEACHERS DESERVE A VOICE

In the business world, Fortune 500 companies are abandoning hierarchy in favor of teamwork, so that employees collaborate, trust each other, and find new ways to solve problems.

What is a major cause for this change? The benefits of people sharing their voices to solve problems on a collaborative team. It's not about checking a box—we can program a machine to do that. It's about creating solutions in a collaborative setting so we can get out-of-the box results.

The same must be true in education.

Not only do teachers deserve their *own* voice, their own opinions and the space to express how they feel, but education will be more effective with their participation.

RAE SAYS

I have spent far too much time sitting in a room, feeling invisible.

I cannot effectively count how many times I have been a teacher in a room surrounded by my colleagues and being "volun-told" I will be taking part in a new pilot or initiative working its way down the pipeline. Curriculum, instructional practices, grading policies—you name it, I've experienced changes that seem to move in and out of a revolving door of discombobulated ideas.

But I am the one in the trenches, striving to implement these ideas with my students. And, more often than not, I can tell you within the first ten minutes of learning about a new initiative if it is going to work in my classroom, because I know my kids.

It continues to baffle me when ideas come from the top down without anyone asking my input—especially when I didn't even realize the dilemma they are striving to solve even existed in my learning environment.

We are doing just fine over here . . . thanks!

Honestly, if they stopped in my classroom once in a while, they'd know that . . .

Implementing a new idea into a classroom without teacher input is like trying to bake a cake without the bowls, spoons, or pans. Regardless of how much you think you know about baking and the steps necessary to get there, you aren't able to create much of anything without the tools you need to get started.

Teachers are in the trenches living the experiences. Teachers are the ones interacting with kids and making the initiatives and support happen. Teachers see firsthand how a certain program or idea impacts students.

So why is it that teachers don't have more say when it comes to professional development, how staff meetings are organized, curricular programs that are implemented, how money is allocated, what types of assemblies happen at school, and so many other decisions that happen at a school?

ADAM SAYS

I have sat in on many principal interviews over the years, and one question that's notoriously asked is "How will you work with staff to bring them all together for a common goal?"

The question has a few different variations but is really asking the same thing. How are you (the leader) going to bring everyone together, listen to what they have to say, take that input and bring that cohesive team together for kids?

Let me tell you, candidates will always say that listening to all voices and opinions is paramount, and that they have a vision of shared decision-making. Leaders say that in interviews, but it doesn't always happen in real life.

Teachers deserve a voice. For us to say that is one thing, and we believe it wholeheartedly. It's now time for you to stand up and let your voice be heard.

It's one thing to be rude, crass, or disrespectful, or to complain just for the sake of complaining. It's another thing to advocate, collaborate, speak up, and voice your educated opinion to the decision-makers you work with.

And trust us when we say that we understand the hesitation to speak up. We've heard too many stories of teachers being told their idea wouldn't work, there isn't enough money in the budget, you're just a teacher and should focus on your classroom, you're too veteran or too young and don't understand the big picture, or you get paid to teach and "we" get paid to make the decisions.

We get it—you've been shot down before and you don't want to go through it again because the experience is no fun.

It's time to try a different approach so your voice is heard loud and clear.

Jesus Huerta

Elementary School Teacher
California

I started off teaching the way some people in my area go into anything: a teacher suggested it. I was a teacher's aide after being asked by my freshman math teacher, Carl Hinshaw. I thought it would be a cake class, but then he eventually asked me to teach a lesson, review with the class, and grade the students' work. He would "read" his newspaper, but I caught him checking on me. Eventually he mentioned that maybe I had a knack for teaching, but I brushed it off . . . and somehow I still ended up here!

My mom was a teacher in Mexico before she immigrated with my dad. She believed that leaving her career behind in Mexico was a better option to come to the States and start a new life. There were many ups and downs, but eventually we were able to be successful because I became a teacher, my brother is a teacher, and my sister is a supervisor for the Housing Authority.

I teach in Calexico, which is located in southern California. This is waaaaay down south in California and is a border town through and through. This impacts the student population significantly because of the socioeconomic situation of students, some traveling back and forth from Mexico to the US regularly, and some students having to live with extended family members. The last one is huge because many of them share a room with multiple cousins and/or siblings. This means they don't have a space of their own to learn in.

I teach because I live in an area where there is no real industry and has students who are impacted socioeconomically. I want to show them that they can learn and give them exposure to the tools of the future. I want them to realize they are capable of so much more, even if they were told in previous years they would not go far.

ONE VOICE VERSUS A UNITED FRONT

First off, people won't hear you as loud when you're talking alone. United with a group, your voice will travel farther and deeper. Talk with your colleagues to get on the same page. There is power in numbers, and many voices coming together are stronger than one by itself. Be pragmatic in your approach and calculated with your timing, and keep the focus on instruction, relationships, and most importantly the kids.

Your voice as an educator is strong and powerful, but do not limit your team by only including educators. Teachers cannot be the only ones beating the drum. Get parents involved, too. School district officials may not like this approach, but it sends a very clear message when teachers and parents are bringing their voices together in an organized and educated way.

ADAM SAYS

When I was a principal, we created a school motto called "Team Kid." Every single person on our staff and in our community knew about "Team Kid." And when you have that level of buy-in participation when it comes to the direction you want to take your school, it's a completely solid and impenetrable united front. If it's an oath you all take, or specific goals that have been agreed upon, together is always better than by yourself.

We could include a long laundry list of different areas where teachers can share their voices, but at the end of the day you know your community best.

Be strategic. Do not choose twenty different things to advocate for. Make your list, and then as a team choose two or three as your key pillars. Consider choosing a big one and two smaller ideas to tackle. It feels good to be successful, and you probably don't want to keep hitting your head against the wall if that one big idea just won't go anywhere or is taking too long.

You have a voice.

Your voice is powerful.

And your voice must be heard.

Because all teachers deserve it, and so do you.

LET THEM MAKE THE CALL

We need to start doing more with teachers.

As we've said, teachers deserve to have a voice in making the call when it comes to curriculum, programs, initiatives, assessments, students, and report cards. You're going to get more out of teachers when you include them in the conversation.

We already know the same is true for students. When we include students in the decision-making process and they take more ownership in the process, they work harder to make the idea into a reality.

RAE SAYS

After years of facilitating a self-paced mastery-focused classroom, I was shocked to see the impact students could make without me handing them the road map to success.

I coached them.

I provided students with a multitude of learning opportunities.

I posed questions to challenge their thinking.

But when it came to students determining their pathway toward mastery, I left a lot of opportunity for students to build their own adventure.

There have been too many stories to count of instances where students went above and beyond in their creativity to build a pathway to learning that far exceeded my expectations as an educator.

Why? Because I gave students the control to make the call.

And I owe it to my leadership, who carried enough trust in me as an educator to make the call of facilitating my classroom in a way that strays from the norm. Their support and faith in my ability allowed me to have the confidence to try something new, encounter failure, get back up, find an outlet to brainstorm, reflect, and then try again.

Jonathan Compas

Kindergarten Teacher
Missouri

You want to know my "why"? Well, it starts with my grandpa, the PE teacher everyone loved and still does to this day. My grandpa gave his students life lessons and experiences they wouldn't forget. He taught generations how to fish and climb the rope, and helped them see how fun life should be. I currently teach in the same school he did all those years ago, and I have his former students' kids and grandkids. The families still talk about him with a smile on their face.

My "why" is easy: I want to give kids the experiences they will remember for a lifetime. I want my kids to leave knowing that school is a place to have fun *and* learn! Schools need to be fun again, and somehow the fun has been lost on some of us as educators. We were all once kids, and we need to remember that school doesn't have to be serious all the time. I want to leave that lasting impression of school being fun and be the teacher that made learning fun. This is my "why."

If you think about it this way, when teachers have the authority to make the call and are also encouraged to make it, they're going to do so more often on their own because they feel supported in their work.

Some leaders will say things like: "We encourage autonomy." "I scheduled a committee meeting, and only five teachers showed up." "We're very collaborative in our decision-making."

But are they doing what they need to be doing? If not enough people show up, then you have to go out to the people. And if you *have* to go out to the people, you're not visible enough in classrooms and schools to actually get to know people.

This isn't a judgment on any leader, it's just what we see happening far too often across the country. If others around us won't change, then we have to change.

ADAM SAYS

When I was a principal my first-grade team came to me with a problem. Too many of their students were struggling with phonics and understanding the basics, which as you can imagine was impacting their reading and overall comprehension.

We met. They told me the problem. They asked if I had any money. I had some.

They asked for my advice. I told them I didn't have any. I said, "You know your students best, you know what they need, you're going to be teaching them whatever the new program is. Find what you need, and I'll find the money and professional development to make it happen and will support you 100 percent."

I could have tried to dance my way around talking about phonics instruction, but I really didn't have anything at all to add to the conversation, so I let my teachers make the call.

They collaborated and researched different programs, I also did some research on the side with other principals to get some background knowledge just in case, and then we all came back together a couple weeks later to plan.

The teachers needed me, they just needed me a lot less than they thought they needed me.

Too many leaders want or need to be needed, and that's not how you're going to get all of your students access to the curriculum. Teachers should 100 percent keep their leadership in the loop about what's going on and any needs that arise. But leaders should stay out of the way unless they see their teachers having trouble or going off course during the process.

With all of this being said, every team is going to be a little bit different. Obviously there's no formula for decision-making, other than putting all the pieces on the table, having a conversation about each one, and then letting your teachers make the call. And sometimes, it's going to be the wrong call, and that's totally okay. But if we never give teachers the opportunity to make the call, they're never going to have the experience of going through the process, learning from their mistakes, and then making a better call that will be the right one next time around.

We want our kids to be empowered to make their own decisions—we have to allow and encourage our teachers to do the same. Let teachers make the call.

Please don't read this chapter and then expect teachers to make all the calls, and do all the work, and implement everything. That's not what we're talking about. What we're saying is give them the destination, and let them draw their own map, because they know the terrain very well.

A simple strategy to build a sustainable model within your classroom or school building is to use this quick seven-step checklist to ensure all the bases have been covered as you work toward building a collaborative plan:

- Identify the problem: What do you want to solve?
- Tap into the benefits: What benefits does this provide and to whom?

- Define your measures: How will success be measured? How will you know it works?
- Prepare the ecosystem: What supports need to be put in place for the entire ecosystem? This includes every element of the school!
- Spitball the challenges: Speak to the fears. What hiccups can you predict and problem-solve around in advance?
- Protect and nurture: Check in with those involved and foster the project. Protect your people and nurture them throughout the process.
- Communicate continually: Communicate, communicate, communicate. Allow everyone to feel up to speed and included in the process—no matter how small!

In addition to letting teachers make the call, we also feel teachers should question the rules.

QUESTION THE RULES

ADAM SAYS

"You're always breaking the rules, Adam. How do you get away with it?"

Truth is, I don't break the rules—I question the rules.

Years ago we wanted to start podcasting with second-grade classes at our school as a way for the kids to project their voices and connect with their parents while at school and with what they were learning. The app we wanted to use was *blocked*. Y'all know what I'm talking about with blocked apps; it basically takes an act of Congress to get it unblocked and loaded on the devices. Well, we could have had the kids record their podcasts on the app through our phone. The phones didn't go through the network and therefore weren't blocked.

We almost went down that route, but I decided to question the rules instead of break them. I reached out to our technology director with the request, and the answer back was a quick and curt no. Didn't ask questions, didn't want to talk—just a no.

So I sent another message and cc'd the superintendent and assistant superintendent with my request and our "why." I questioned why this app was blocked when all we wanted to do was help project student voices under the direct supervision of the teacher.

I invited everyone to come and see firsthand what the app was and how we were going to integrate it with students into the curriculum.

Fast-forward a few days and we got approval. Breaking rules may be faster sometimes, but questioning them will be more beneficial in the long run!

Breaking the rules can be dangerous and isn't something we would advise doing on a regular basis. Once you get labeled as a rule breaker, the leash your higher-ups might be holding onto gets shorter and shorter and shorter.

In our experience, people who choose to break the rules get in trouble a lot, and then they're not able to do much of anything when it comes to change, innovation, or new ideas. So, don't break—*question*!

When it comes to education, so many of the things we do are because of insanely archaic mindsets, or regulations, or even board policies that just haven't been updated in decades. We've seen board policies from the 1970s; they've been photocopied so many times you can barely read what it says because the text has faded so much. And those policies need to be questioned. Those rules that haven't changed need to be questioned. The procedures have to be looked at because if they aren't helping teachers in their classrooms, they need to be questioned and then changed!

For example, why do schools have hour-long staff meetings every month that everyone needs to attend? Why can't students take devices home if they don't have access at home? Why do veteran teachers make so much more than newer teachers just because they have longevity? Why do principals need to attend school board meetings every month, and why do they sometimes go until 11:00 p.m.?

Why, why, why, why, why, why, why?

Every school district has these issues, and it's time to start asking why!

ADAM SAYS

When I was a principal, there were so many ambiguous rules that we had to follow, for reasons that made zero sense at all.

We bought every teacher a MacBook Air to use at school and at home.

District said we couldn't.

Why? Because it had never been done before.

No other teachers in the district except the ones at my school had laptops, and this was in 2012. Of course it had never been done before—because teachers never had them before.

I shouldn't have even asked if we could send them home—but you don't want to get a bad reputation. So I talked about it with my supervisor, and she was cool with it for so many obvious reasons. The number one reason was that it was 2012 and half the world had laptops. Others at our central office didn't like the idea, but I didn't care.

It was good for teachers.

Which means it was good for students.

We continued to question and got the permission we needed.

Question the rules and write some new ones! Don't be afraid, be excited. Don't be shy. Stand up and speak up. Don't say your voice doesn't count—it does. Don't wait for someone else to question the rules—you can do that.

Make sure you are heard, question the rules, and make the call. It's time!

#TEACHERSDESERVEIT EDUCATOR EXPERIMENT

1. What do you want to shout from the rooftops? Every educator deserves to be heard—and we want you to share your voice today! What is one idea you've had for school that you're passionate about?

Write a paragraph about it and tweet it at us with the hashtag #TeachersDeserveIt. Use your voice and start a conversation!

2. It's time to start asking *why*! What rule or procedure needs a face lift? Share out the rule and ask others to share their updated policies or procedures. Use #TeachersDeserveIt to ensure your network sees your message and you get the updated ideas you need to give a facelift to your least favorite rule.

3. What's one idea you've had that you need parent or community support for? Write up the idea and share it using #TeachersDeserveIt. Share it with parents and your community on your website, your newsletter, or in an email.

CHAPTER 3
Teachers Deserve Community Validation

It's imperative for the community to see our jobs aren't a walk in the park. Teachers don't deserve negativity, but instead celebration for the work they do on a daily basis to change students' lives. We must choose to educate the public about what we do. This is how we can begin to reduce the hatred and increase the appreciation of educators as a whole. We can start this right now by showing appreciation to our fellow teachers—and we owe it to each other to begin modeling this practice.

Finally, we must call for more larger-scale community celebrations like Ellen does on her TV show! Well, because how awesome would that be?

TEACHERS DESERVE FOR OTHERS TO SEE IT AIN'T EASY

It doesn't matter what you teach, where you teach, or why you teach—this job is not just a career field, it's an all-encompassing lifestyle.

RAE SAYS

Let's take this week . . . I am currently sitting in a Starbucks on a Saturday afternoon. I won't lie, this stool is making my tush sore (since I've been here for three hours) and the vanilla latte I ordered is long gone. Maybe I should go grab another to get through the massive to-do list I have . . .

I am not sure how you all do it, but I essentially live by two key organizational systems: Google Calendar and my green Moleskine notebook. If the event is not in my calendar, it doesn't exist, and if the task is not on my to-do list, then trust me, it has already escaped from my mind. There is just too much to do!

Between the balance of lesson planning, providing timely feedback, parent contacts, and administration emails, a forty-five-minute planning period does not even skim the surface of what I need to address these needs.

But, like everything, it all takes time.

Teaching ain't easy.

It's challenging to explain why this career is difficult. We face challenges that require a lot of strength, like helping students in crisis. And while working with students facing learning disabilities, our intellectual insight can be put to the test as we work toward the right solution. All these things make our work very difficult and require a lot of emotional strength, intellectual finesse, and endurance.

This can also be true as we complete tasks around the house, deal with life's challenges, or set a desired fitness goal for the new year. However, it is really true, almost daily, for an educator. We need the larger community to understand that about us.

This is not to say the struggle outweighs the result. We think most educators would argue their opportunity to help shape a student's future has a meaningful impact, but this drive competes with the continued stress of the educational field.

For example, teachers often clock over twelve hours of work throughout the day—entering their school building before dawn and leaving after sunset. So, it stings when the community sees us as lazy and opportunistic.

RAE SAYS

I was at dinner a few months ago with a few professionals in the business field. Our conversations were refreshing and, because they were in a different field, went beyond lesson planning and student needs.

The conversation shifted when someone at the table asked me if I liked my job.

"Of course!" I responded with a huge smile on my face.

"I assumed so," he muttered, sitting back in his chair. "It must be awesome having your summers off!"

I bit my tongue, took a deep breath, and debated with myself about the proper response. Needless to say, I was not going to allow that comment to go unaddressed.

It hurts when we work so hard and the community's main perception of us is that we "get summers off," especially when so many people can't handle the stress of the job and have to leave it.

According to *Forbes* in 2019, a third of educators drop out of the field after five years in the classroom. While there are countless reasons for this, one continues to be true: those who enter into the field and believe it's easy to be a teacher don't stay in it for long.

Trust me, "summers off" is not enough of an enticing feature.

The truth is, the hard work that exists in the world is the heart work. Our work requires an exceptionally strong and passion-driven individual to enter into a situation where their patience will be tested, their strength will be assessed, their insight will be challenged, and their heart will be broken all in the hope of serving.

It's time to begin seeing educators for the heroes they are! Because without them, where would our students be?

IT'S NOT ENOUGH TO HOPE

They don't know. They—your mother, your neighbor, your dentist, the clerk at the bank, that Target employee—don't know all that you do. They are ignorant to the initiatives on your shoulders and all the student concerns bubbling up.

It's not their fault. It's partly ours.

The reason many do not understand the heart work going on in the world of education is because educators have become famous for their silence. We cannot hope for others to understand the challenge that is teaching—hope is not a strategy. Let's make a plan and do what we do best—educate.

Because in reality, it never stops. You know the feeling—just when that sense of "I've got a handle on everything" appears, something else pops up that needs your attention.

A new student transferred into your class, and they're two grade levels behind on their reading and math, and your school doesn't have any spots open for pull-out intervention. What do you do?

Or your principal is starting a new committee to look at social and emotional well-being, and they want you to join—even though you're already on a few other committees and don't really have time for a myriad of reasons.

Hope is not enough; we need the community to know teaching just ain't easy.

THE RIGHT MESSAGE

There are two ways to share the challenges with teaching. One involves complaining in the hope of garnering sympathy and shifting blame, while the other involves educating in the hope of recruiting resources for more support.

Carly Spina

Bilingual Third-Grade Teacher
Illinois

I serve a beautiful, linguistically diverse community. They are my "why." I want all my kids and families to have equal access and opportunity. I see my role as that of a connector. I know that I'm needed as an advocate in my community for those I serve. I sometimes must ask the difficult questions, challenge fixed mindsets, or push thinking forward—which isn't always easy, but I know that my role and my impact are bigger than what's inside my comfort zone.

The district I'm currently serving has vast socioeconomic diversity. We have families who own multiple homes in multiple states, while other families save up money to rent a movie for the weekend. The usual "What did you do this summer?" conversation many folks have upon the onset of a new school year activity demonstrates the privilege gap in obvious ways, and the activity itself makes me cringe.

Until the make-up of our PTAs actually represents all of the parents and guardians in the community, I will continue to push. Until the folks at the decision-making table represent my students and families, I will continue to ask. Until the curriculum shares the stories and histories of all, I will continue to question. Until the documents we send home are available and accessible in multiple languages, I will continue to demand high-quality translations not generated by technology.

My voice means nothing if I'm not using it to serve others. My hands are meaningless if I'm not holding the doors open to welcome folks in. My feet are pointless if I'm not supporting the forward movement of a system. If I go home at the end of the day and question whether or not I was brave enough to ask the hard question in a meeting, challenge a perspective, or address an assumed privilege, then I have to ask myself, why am I even at the table?

Complaining is not a strategy—we must be solution-oriented in our approach.

Teachers are not martyrs.

Starting *today*, begin having a hundred conversations about your job. Share your story with friends, neighbors, and your connections on social media. Write a letter to your local government official entailing what your job is like on the daily. Start a podcast with a colleague to celebrate and share your message.

It's your message and you're in charge of it, so don't let someone else speak for you.

Stand up. Plug in that microphone. Share your story. Share your message. Share your triumphs. And most importantly—keep it real. People deserve to hear the truth; that's the only way we'll see real and lasting change.

TEACHERS DESERVE CELEBRATION, NOT HATE

It's not enough for the community just to see that teaching ain't easy. They also need to learn that we don't deserve the hate we're given and instead deserve to be celebrated!

Everyone knows the song "Shake It Off" by Taylor Swift knocking how all the haters are gonna hate! We know you are already humming the tune in your head, trying to remember the epic dance moves from the video, which was viewed over two billion times on YouTube. But what's the major takeaway from this catchy 2014 pop song?

Don't be a hater!

Teachers deserve encouragement and celebration for the work they are doing!

RAE SAYS

I will always remember the day I walked into my first Institute Day as a new teacher. It was hosted in the district's high school auditorium, and the stress of deciding where to sit drove me to show up far too early for a meeting most of the community was not so eager to attend.

As the teachers were welcomed into the new school year, Ron Clark walked onto the stage to set the tone for the event. Wow, was his energy infectious!

Not having been connected to him prior, I was blown away by his charisma, energy, and passion. His dedication seemed to ooze off the stage as he moved through the aisles and crowd. During his session, he asked my principal to join him on stage. Ron spoke about the impact celebrating a teacher could have on their ability to reach students and act as a good staff member.

Suddenly, Ron Clark asked my principal to choose a teacher to celebrate. As he scanned the room and made eye contact with me, my heart stopped beating. It was such an honor to be celebrated in front of my colleagues. It was such an honor to be celebrated by my principal.

And to be completely transparent, it was *that* moment, not three months into teaching, that I started believing I could do well as an educator.

And I owe it all to Ron Clark, who created the culture of celebration and for Mr. Thompson, my principal, who believed in my abilities enough to choose me for that moment.

Now obviously Ron Clark can't do this for every school across the country, but you can. You can celebrate your colleagues. We shouldn't be waiting around for someone else to take the microphone and speak up. You can speak up. You can start the conversation. You can create a tradition of celebration and encouragement that should be a tradition in every school and workplace around the world.

And without even knowing it, you know what some of the people in the crowd that day were thinking? *Why did Rae get chosen to be celebrated in front of everybody?*

The haters.

Life is too dang short—and teaching is too dang hard. Negativity along with hate doesn't bring any positivity into your life. Don't listen to the haters, or the naysayers, or the people in the corner whispering and pointing fingers at you or others. To be truthful, we feel sorry for those people and really hope they somehow find happiness in their lives.

And here's what you can do. You can stay positive, because the only place to go when others go low is high. Don't allow that negativity to creep into your life. Don't allow the side comments to affect how you feel and what you do in your classroom with your students and your colleagues, because what someone else thinks of you doesn't even matter.

The people that you choose to surround yourself with are the ones that do matter. And we get it, maybe you're in a department or grade level with some teachers that you don't get along with or just simply don't like. We get it. The trick is to be so positive and kind and energetic and celebratory that you are just oozing with so much goodness, and the negativity and hate don't even have a chance to enter your ecosystem.

It's hard to do at times, we get it. Get your mind to a place where it's easy, because that's really the only choice you have to make.

Teachers deserve encouragement.

Teachers deserve celebration.

Teachers deserve to be treated like they really matter, because you really do.

Teachers deserve colleagues that treat them how they would want to be treated—that is not too much to ask. It can also be as simple as a compliment. Encouragement and celebration take many forms.

There is enough celebration and happiness to go around for everyone!

ADAM SAYS

When I was a principal, we tried really hard at doing things that had always been done a certain way—in a different way.

One such activity was staff meetings. The staff meetings at our school had always taken place in the staff room, and it was not the best location. I just wanted something different.

So we started holding our monthly staff meetings in a different teacher's classroom each month. This may sound like a small change, but small changes add up to large dividends when they're done with the right intention. Teachers would clean up their rooms in anticipation of their colleagues coming over. It gave them a sense of pride each month and also led to additional collaboration among teachers that normally wouldn't collaborate.

The most profound impact this small change had was what I had everyone do as they left the meeting each month. Every teacher was given a Post-it note and had to write a compliment about the teacher whose room we were in. Short, simple, free, and so impactful.

Words matter because people remember them. They're important. Compliments are contagious when done with purpose.

#ComplimentATeacher today. Brighten their day, and let's help everyone feel just a little bit better!

You deserve it!

TEACHERS DESERVE MORE ELLEN

We don't know about you, but we both think Ellen DeGeneres is pretty awesome to teachers. Have you ever seen one of her huge giveaways to a lucky teacher on her show?

Ellen, a TV host, best-selling author, and celebrity icon, has a talk show that airs every weekday. Each episode for over seventeen seasons, she celebrates incredible stories around the world—meeting her mission of spreading kindness. Popular guests on her show have included geography genius four-year-olds, millionaires donating funds to those less fortunate, and passionate teachers.

Laurie McIntosh

Kindergarten Teacher
Alberta, Canada

Being a teacher after being an educational assistant for five years was literally a dream come true. I completed my education degree during some of the hardest years of my life. If it weren't for the incredible teachers, administrators, and family members I had surrounding me, I never would have gone back to get that degree, much less finish it. When I entered the classroom, I vowed to do whatever I could to make *every* child feel included and loved in our classroom. I am still grateful every day to have the title of "teacher." I do not take the title lightly.

I am fourteen years in, and most days I still lie in bed first thing in the morning and smile at the experiences and activities, but most of all the connections, I am planning for our learners. I love connecting them to their community. Any chance I get to have them meet or collaborate with another caring human on this planet, who encourages them and believes in them and loves them as much as I do? That's what drives me. That's what makes all of this worth it to me. That's what keeps me in the game.

I have gone through some major shifts in thinking and priorities in my career. One of the biggest ones came after appearing on *The Ellen Show* twice in 2015. My life was instantly and forever changed in the most wonderful way possible. To feel seen, heard, and affirmed by my idol was an incredibly powerful experience that greatly impacted my awareness of my own "why" as an educator. Furthermore, it gave me the strength and confidence to unapologetically and relentlessly speak and live this "why" in an authentic way in our classroom. When I need to be inspired? I only need to look back and watch that episode to remind me of my "why." It always helps me remember that I am enough and what truly matters to me as a teacher.

Shortly after my appearance on the show, I started becoming much more invested in our learners' dreams, not as adults but right now, as four-, five-, and six-year-olds in our kindergarten classroom. I started to make much more mindful and thoughtful attempts to essentially be *their* Ellen.

After reading a book one day about a certain pigeon wanting to drive a certain bus, one little one raised his hand excitedly saying, "Mrs. Mac! Mrs. Mac! Do you know that I want to be a bus driver one day? I can't *wait* to see what the view looks like from that bus seat!" He was so enthusiastic about this dream, and every chance he got he would repeat his bus driver dream and draw the view that he thought he would see from up there. Ultimately, his dream led to us to lessons on persuasive writing, letter writing, and gratitude. We *all* wrote letters to the bus driver explaining all the reasons we were grateful for him and his service and all the reasons we thought he should visit our school. Lo and behold, one special Tuesday morning we heard a honk outside our classroom window and saw the bus driver waving us on from the sidewalk. The kids squealed and screamed with excitement, running to the classroom door. Were they excited for the bus? Absolutely. But they were even more excited for their friend.

"The bus is here, A!"

"Your dream is going to come true today, A!"

"Let A go first since *he* is the one who got that bus to come here today!"

Oh. My. Heart. I often reflect on that bus story. A simple way we took one child's dream and made it happen together. *That* is my why.

To guide our learners (and myself!) through experiences of kindness and collaboration that connect us to our community and validate our ability to be leaders in our world. Coming together each and every day as a team to dream big and work to make those dreams come true helps me to see, hear, and affirm our learners as valued leaders, just as my idol did for me. I am grateful each and every day for the gift I am given to live my "why" in our classroom and in our community.

Sometimes teachers are surprised at their home early in the morning with a camera crew and all their colleagues from work. The teacher is caught at the door just before leaving and then bombarded with money, gift cards, supplies, and endless other treats for their class. Additionally, gifts are provided to celebrate the teacher. These often include funds for the teacher's family or a vacation at a beautiful resort.

Who does not enjoy a tear-jerking teacher story about an educator doing everything in their power to impact their students' lives? Their self-sacrificing story is inspiring not only to other educators but to millions of viewers.

We can't imagine how amazing that must make a teacher feel. Not only for the celebratory excitement of winning cool prizes and cash or meeting a fabulous celebrity, but for the acknowledgment of the hard work teachers put in every day. It must feel amazing to be seen.

Ellen is also known to bring teachers onto her show. Sitting in that white comfy chair next to the host herself, teachers glow as they share their educational journey on the iconic stage. Often Ellen has been shown a video the teacher has made about their class, or something extra special the teacher has done with students that has some really great "wow" factor. So, Ellen wants to celebrate them with her entire audience.

And you know what—teachers need more Ellen.

To support teachers in financial ways and to make them feel extra special.

To tell the world about the special and meaningful work they're doing for the students in their class.

To harness the power of large companies and corporations in recognizing them for doing the work that is so important for our country and the next generation.

We need more people like Ellen.

And while we know there is only one Ellen, there have to be others out there that want to emulate how she celebrates educators.

RAE SAYS

I had a student teacher once ask me if she could miss a school day because she had won tickets to *The Ellen Show*.

How could you even argue with her? One day of a yearlong student teaching gig missed for a once-in-a-lifetime visit to a show I watch on my phone each afternoon? Go for it!

When she got back from her trip, she was over the moon.

She couldn't stop talking about the energy.

She couldn't stop talking about the laughter.

She couldn't stop talking about the incredible stories she was exposed to.

And she couldn't stop talking about the presence Ellen had as she interacted with her audience and echoed the message of kindness to her viewers.

Let's bring more Ellen into our schools and communities by making it our mission to make the world a little brighter.

How about partnering with your local Rotary Club to highlight a different teacher in your community on a weekly basis? The Rotarians can make the weekly trip to a different school and surprise a teacher with coffee, a gift card, banners, and signs. We realize it's not feasible to give away all that Ellen does, and that's okay, but we know we can do better.

Start a YouTube channel that is strictly focused on celebrating teachers in your building. Assign students to the YouTube team, and have them make a two-to-three-minute video that highlights the teachers and their accomplishments. On a weekly basis it gets pushed out through the channel and other social media accounts.

Choose one teacher a month and have multiple leaders from the central office take over their classroom at different times to give them a break. This allows the teacher to take some time for themselves, and it also gets those district leaders in classrooms and interacting with kids. Directors, assistant superintendents, and even the superintendent should be involved with this. And you know what else: it doesn't cost the district any money at all. But the goodwill and visibility it brings far outweigh the cost of those individuals' time.

Bring your classes together for some collaboration. Institute High-Five Friday and get people smiling and feeling more special.

Get up and dance. Blast the music. Be kind to one another.

Because teachers deserve it!

#TEACHERSDESERVEIT EDUCATOR EXPERIMENT

Tell five people this week about what your job is like as a teacher. Every time you share it, post about it using the hashtag #TeachersDeserveIt.

CHAPTER 4

Teachers Deserve Recognition of Their Expertise

Teachers deserve to be seen as the experts they are. Not because they went to college and have a credential, but because they spent countless hours building and designing lessons that kids will dig and want to be a part of. Now it doesn't just stop at lesson design and credibility; teachers can increase their impact by choosing to interact with the public in a positive way. Assuming positive intentions is key when building relationships and being the experts they are.

One way to help boost that impression with parents is by using student voice. We talked about students at Adam's school creating podcasts in a previous chapter, and that project turned out to be positive for student development and community involvement! We must act like the professionals we are and build solid relationships with the parent community.

And please, if you have any pent-up negativity toward parents and the community, let it go. It's only going to bring you down a path that has no positive outcome. When they go low, we go high, because that's the best place to be!

YOU DESERVE TO BE VIEWED AS AN EXPERT

At what point are you an expert?

Spending forty-five minutes on the phone with a parent who believes you are unintelligent and "out to get" their child is mind numbing. You sit in your chair, ear pressed up against the phone attached to the wall, and calmly listen to a parent question your choices, intelligence, intentions, and focus as an educator.

"I think you should . . ." or "I don't understand why you don't just . . ." are the phrases muttered by a frustrated parent questioning your decisions as an educator.

You know you'd never say it—because you are a professional—but you always think to yourself : *I've been doing this for a long time. I have impacted thousands of students in my career. I went to school to do this work effectively. How are YOU an expert?*

Teachers deserve to be viewed as the experts they are.

Every day is a new opportunity to grow. A new opportunity to reach a student who was once viewed as unreachable and to challenge a student who was overlooked or underserved. Every day is a chance to provide students the opportunity to master a topic and take their knowledge to educate their community. And yet, it seems every day teachers are the ones overlooked as the "people on the ground" preparing our youth for a future we don't even know yet.

Now, of course, demanding to be seen as an expert isn't enough on its own. This title must be earned and proven over and over and over again. Nevertheless, the evidence is there—minus the few who may be stealing the show and giving teachers a bad rep.

Have you been on Facebook on a Sunday evening before? It can be toxic sometimes!

The truth is you have the power to craft your News Feed to look however you choose.

Hans and Jennifer Appel

Middle School Counselor and Middle School Innovation Coach
Washington

Having spent the past two decades working side by side to shape middle school minds and hearts, it's easy to overlook the personal and professional growth that has led to our intense joy. Truth be told, we come from very different backgrounds; Jen is a fourth-generation educator born to be a high-impact learning leader, and Hans is a high-ACE child of trauma who used school as a powerful escape from his challenging upbringing. As high school sweethearts, we found ourselves quite literally growing up together while we began our path toward serving others. While our stories couldn't have been more different for the first seventeen years, we've gladly embraced a unified story to positively disrupt education with our brand of intentional influence.

We've been given the rare chance of working together on our life's passion. As a counselor and a teacher working at the same school, we've had a common language, mission, and vision for exercising our whole-child efforts. Waking up each day with your best friend, energized to reach the same community of adolescents, has fueled our daily joy. However, over the past five years, we've discovered an additional adventure to pour gasoline on this already white-hot flame of purpose. Through speaking, writing, and creating original school culture content, we're now sharing our award-winning work with educators around the world. And by broadening our impact, our commitment to this work has only been strengthened.

We believe that education—at its *highest* level—is about helping others discover and develop their *joy*! Isn't that what life is all about? Understanding our own unique strengths and passions and aligning those to some deeper meaning leaves us filled with purpose. Our "why" is to help students and staff forever *shatter* the ceiling on culture and climate by magnifying the lens to real sustainable *joy*!

Don't enjoy seeing your family complain about their new diet program or sell you wrinkle-erasing lotion? Click the Unfollow button, and it's as good as gone.

The problem is when you have people you care about who choose to post negative things when Sunday rolls around.

"Ugh. I don't want to teach tomorrow."

"Why is the weekend over? Don't make me go back!"

"I can't wait until Friday because I am done with these kids this year."

Real talk: these comments are a part of the problem as to why we can't be seen as experts. An expert wouldn't paint such a profession *this* important to the future success of our world in this way.

Could you imagine if you had a surgery Monday morning and your doctor wrote this post: "Ugh, so bummed the weekend is over. I really don't want to go to work tomorrow. I am far too tired!"

Yikes. Are you still feeling confident for your surgery in less than eight hours?

To earn the title of "expert," we must educate our friends, family, and outside networks on the impact and real lifestyle of an educator. We are not whining, underpaid 9-to-5 workers. We may be underpaid, but we hustle, we have grit, we set the bar high, and we exceed expectations.

How do we send this message? Well, there are a number of different ways to get started, but to put it simply, we must begin the process the same way we do with our students: connect, share, reflect, build relationships, and provide opportunities for re-teaching.

STUDENT VOICES

Change takes a village effort. Utilize your students to echo the message of your impact.

In your next unit, don't just provide your students with dynamic learning opportunities, but explain the "why" throughout the process. Send a weekly email home or (Rae's personal favorite) send a video email.

Better yet, take it one step further by asking your students to utilize a tech tool that connects directly to their parents for daily reflection and goal setting.

RAE SAYS

In my classroom, my students operate within a framework that allows them to master content at their own pace. Throughout this process, it is essential for students to reflect and goal-set during each work session to effectively identify how their learning is going, where they are finding they still need support, and what their plan of action is.

When I began this approach, students went through the goal-setting and reflection process on a piece of paper. After running into numerous issues, I shifted to a web-based tool that allowed me to connect each student's account to their specific parents. This shift allowed each parent access to a portal into their students' daily learning each and every day, 180 days a year.

When I communicate the "why" and methods of learning to students throughout their learning process, they communicate the "why" and methods of learning back into their reflections.

While I still found myself striving to communicate with parents to explain new methods being used in the classroom, I was often interrupted by stakeholders sharing that they already knew this information because their eleven-year-old shared it in their reflection last week.

Too much communication is a good problem to have.

CJ Reynolds

High School English and History of Hip-Hop Teacher
Pennsylvania

I went to one of the toughest high schools in southern New Jersey. I've seen kids thrown out windows in the lunchroom, beaten with pipes, and jumped for cutting in the front of someone in the lunch line. For me, high school was not a place that focused on academic success, but rather a place to be survived. I was an insecure, quiet, baby-faced kid that struggled to learn. In class I stayed awake and attentive, not because I loved school but because I had to watch my back. Not paying attention to your surroundings could lead to having your backpack or lunch stolen, having gum put in your hair, or getting jabbed with someone's pencil. Teachers never asked if I needed help because I was quiet and looked attentive. Most of their focus went either to the kids that were super smart and actually wanted to engage in class or the kids that were the biggest discipline problems in class. C– students like me flew under the radar, got beat up in the bathroom, and longed to find a place to fit in.

So, one of the most important reasons I became an educator was to be that teacher I always needed when I was a kid. As a teacher, I spend my days making sure students that feel invisible know they are visible. I find students that feel like outsiders and give them a place to belong. I've worked to create a classroom where all students feel comfortable. My kids and I eat breakfast and lunch together every day and talk about what they are interested in. We discuss their struggles, dreams, and concerns. I sit with kids in their hurt and take their interests and turn them into lesson hooks. I know more about video games, superhero movies, and hip-hop music than any other forty-year-old that I know.

After a decade and a half in the classroom, I've learned that it is not our advice but our attention that really matters. I teach because I want my students to know that they are not alone. That they are important, and their lives have value. I want them to know that they belong everywhere.

LET YOUR WALLS DO THE TALKING

Degrees, badges, and micro-credentials are popping up all over as ways for people to share passions and expertise with the world. You can see these images displayed at the bottom of email signatures or in the corners of profile pictures. But why do these celebratory awards only exist virtually or if someone asks?

RAE SAYS

It always confused me that educators did not display their undergraduate and graduate degrees on the walls of their classrooms.

When I had shoulder surgery during the summer of 2019, every four weeks for five months I sat in an exam room waiting to check in with my doctor. On the wall Dr. Li displayed his undergraduate degree, graduate degree, doctoral degree, and the multiple certifications he had earned throughout his twenty-plus-year career.

When I was in middle school, I was told I would most likely not have scores high enough to be considered "college bound" because my learning disability was "too severe."

To be honest, my desire to go to college at that point in my life had nothing to do with wanting to chase a dream, but more to do with status.

Where I grew up, you went to college. This was such a prevalent idea, the community published students' names each May in the newspaper listing their college selection. I *had* to go!

After I got into a four-year university and graduated, that certificate was more than the exit ticket I needed to earn a full-time teaching position. It was a badge of honor. I later received my master's degree and became a professor in the middle-level program a few years later.

Friends, I worked my tush off for those opportunities.

So, I always wondered . . . if this was so important to my parents, my community, my employers, and myself, why was it "uncommon" or "unacceptable" to hang these degrees in my classroom for the world to see?

Teachers are always learning! Show it off!

College degrees, Google certifications, Teach Better Academy course completions, or ISTE Awards—we don't care what it is, celebrate it!

Fill a shelf with moments of your learning to model your continued growth toward betterment for your students! And then, when a family joins you in your classroom for a conference, feel free to talk about your perseverance and passion when you are asked.

Share your struggles. Share your successes. Share your expertise.

Go out, right now, and buy a frame.

TEACHERS DESERVE THE BENEFIT OF THE DOUBT

It's not always the teacher's fault. Teachers also deserve the benefit of the doubt from parents, administration, colleagues, and the community. Teachers are experts and professionals, and giving us the benefit of the doubt is part of that recognition.

RAE SAYS

I was listening to my favorite morning show out of Chicago, and the discussion shifted. The host asked listeners to call in and share their biggest frustrations.

Listeners called in with numerous funny frustrations, ranging from morning traffic to wives leaving hair in the sink drain. But then a parent called in to gripe about Common Core math.

Oh boy . . .

The parent went on and on, sharing their frustration with teachers having endless requirements and the parent feeling helpless at home as things were "just not done this way" when they were in school.

Then the dreaded line came through the radio after the host asked a follow-up question. "I don't know, Eric, I blame the teachers!" the caller said.

There is a common phrase about the teachers in the classroom as those "in the trenches." Teachers in the trenches see education firsthand, every day. They experience initiatives that come and go. They experience student issues as they arise. They plan, reflect, and adjust lessons at a moment's notice. They cover classes when substitutes cannot be found, and they give up their lunch when a child needs reading intervention.

So, when parent emails do not get replied to within twenty-four hours, when phone calls are made while families are still at work, when an idea is only communicated one time at the beginning of the week and the reminder notice never makes it home, teachers deserve the benefit of the doubt.

Additionally, when new plans come down the educational pipeline, educators are often the first in line to tell the community about the change in plans. Hey—don't blame the messenger!

RAE SAYS

A few months ago, I was invited to speak at a church about standards-based grading. The format was described as an open Q&A for families to better understand the SBG concept.

As the seats filled with students and their parents, I was curious how I was going to support this group with understanding the new grading initiative implemented just a few years prior in the public schools.

I won't lie—the initial conversation was quite heated with students and parents talking over one another as they voiced their frustration with the confusion sparked by the new grading system. I sat back and listened as the conversation circled the room, blaming teachers for adding confusion and unrealistic expectations to their students' success.

One parent even added that their child may not be able to get into college because the system was adding so much confusion to the transcript when applying to colleges that only accepted the traditional letter-grade model.

Once the group had felt heard and began to recognize the negative tailspin the conversation had been led into, I took over by clarifying a few ideas they had voiced confusion with. What did we land on?

The shift causing the families such anxiety dealt with three major factors:

1. Poor communication home
2. Speedy implementation
3. Teachers learning the process as it was being implemented rather than prior to the rollout.

So was this really the teachers' fault? Or were there other factors, and did teachers deserve a little benefit of the doubt?

Every chapter in this book focuses on something teachers deserve in an effort to support teachers in understanding they are heard, valued, and have the ability to control the narrative. But this chapter includes a different message, one that is rather simple.

As we find ourselves frustrated with a teacher and quick to judge, it's important to understand that all people, teachers included, deserve the benefit of the doubt.

Everyone has their own battles they are working through that you are not aware of.

Our students.

Our parents.

Our administration.

Our community leaders.

And yes, our teachers.

So, it's important as we bubble up with frustration to stop ourselves from assuming the worst and instead dedicate ourselves to giving each other the benefit of the doubt and strive to understand.

Imagine a world where we listened to understand rather than listened to respond.

You deserve the benefit of the doubt.

#TEACHERSDESERVEIT EDUCATOR EXPERIMENT

1. It's time to hang up your degree! Go hunt down all of the accreditations you have worked on, badges, and awards. Find a spot in your students' learning space and display your credentials proudly! Share your new display to your favorite social platform using #TeachersDeserveIt for others to see!

2. What are you currently holding on to with frustration or resistance? Could you choose to give this the benefit of the doubt and focus more on learning to better understand? Share your current hurdle using #TeachersDeserveIt to see if others can help you better provide the benefit of the doubt and open your mind to new ideas.

3. It's time to send the right message out to our communities to boost the public's perception of the work we do every day as educators. Why not begin today? Share out three moments of your day today. (Psst! Give them all a positive twist!) You may choose to share these via email to families, on social media to your network, or on your teacher website. Allow others to gain a lens into the work you do and the impact you have on students.

   Example: Ms. Hughart's three-moment recap:

   Today I had the opportunity to see a student have a lightbulb moment over long division! I love those moments!

   I spent forty-five minutes making copies for next week, but oh boy was it worth it! We have some exciting learning opportunities coming up soon. (Stay tuned!)

The opportunity to speak with a parent on the phone during my planning period was so productive! I so appreciate the partnership I have with my families to support their students' success!

4. Sundays are challenging, so let's work together to control the narrative! For the next four Sundays, choose to intentionally post something positive on social media. Focus on what makes you excited to start the week! Let's shower our news feeds with excitement!

CHAPTER 5

Teachers Deserve Good Leaders

We're just going to say it—teachers deserve good leadership to support them. That shouldn't even be something that teachers need to ask for, it should just be what teachers get, but we all know that isn't always the case. Leaders need to keep teachers informed about what the larger plan is and what the bigger goals are, because when they do, teachers feel more like they're an integral part of the team. It's also vitally important that teachers develop their own leadership skills, because when those skills are tested and they grow, they'll know more of what it's actually like to be a leader.

ADAM SAYS

People will often say it's easy to forget what being in school was like. Especially if it's been ten or fifteen years since they were last in the classroom. But let me tell you how very important it is to remember.

Years ago, I was a teacher in a public school and usually had no idea what the plan was.

Now don't get me wrong: We had the curriculum that was supposed to be taught. My grade-level team would meet on a weekly basis to discuss assignments, projects, kids, and activities that were happening.

But something was just missing.

As I look back on my time spent in the classroom now, since I've become a principal and director, I know what was missing.

We didn't know what the big picture was.

All of the pieces for the puzzle may very well have been out on the table, but the bigger perspective, the meaning, and, to use a term from the military, our "battle plan" wasn't clear.

Each of the individual units (grade levels and teachers) may have known what they were supposed to be doing, but the lack of connection between us all left me, at least, in the dark on what the plan was.

TEACHERS DESERVE TO KNOW WHAT THE PLAN IS

Teachers deserve to know from their leadership what the plan is and why they're doing it. Teachers don't have to agree on every single part of the plan, but they need to see the big picture of what's happening and why.

When teachers know the plan:

- They're more invested.
- They'll make better decisions that are based on the plan and not the individual success of their grade level or classroom.
- There's a unified message to all stakeholders about the plan and how it's going to be executed.
- They have a compass to use when navigating changes and situations that aren't expected when implementing the plan.

Teachers need to know the plan from their leaders, because when they do, it will be rolled out with so much more efficiency and fidelity if their voice has been heard and they've been consulted along the way. A great way to lose time and money when implementing a plan is to *not* ask the people who are doing the work with students in classrooms every day for input.

ADAM SAYS

Throughout my career in public education, people always told me I talked a lot more and gave them more information than most people. Along the way I was constantly reflecting on comments like those and wondering if I needed to tighten up my dialogue at times.

But as I think back to my time as a classroom teacher, I was constantly keeping my students updated on happenings around campus with construction projects, new teachers that had joined the team, upcoming assignments, and long-term projects that were coming up or that maybe were just ideas in my brain and not yet something that was actually going to happen.

And you know what they did.

They prepared.

They gave me feedback.

They told me which ideas were good and which ideas were bad.

They were open and honest and, in the end, helped me when I had to make a final decision on something.

And when that final decision was made, they were on board because they'd been kept in constant communication the entire time.

You can go down the road by yourself, or you can be open and transparent, and others will come along with you.

We can't tell you how many staff meetings we've attended where the majority of the room had absolutely no clue what was going on because there was no clear objective being discussed. Our staff at school was constantly left in the dark by their leaders and informed of new programs days before they were meant to be implemented, and with minimal to zero input from us, the educators. This system has never made much sense.

We are not exclusively blaming the principals for this miscommunication. Rather, this stems from a bigger issue often sparked from central office administrators being completely out of touch with what is happening in our classrooms with teachers and students on a daily basis.

Nevertheless, the disconnect that exists between closed-door office meetings and where the teachers are, in the trenches, is one we can no longer overlook.

ADAM SAYS

A good friend of mine was telling me a story about how his third-grade son was given a reading assessment and then identified as needing intervention. Both he and his wife were surprised at the assessment result because their son had been a strong reader for years.

They went along with the school's assessment, sent their son to intervention, and very abruptly, just a couple of weeks later, he was exited from the program.

The note home said, "He's doing great, awesome comprehension and doesn't need intervention any longer."

When my friend was telling me this story, my brain was searching for an answer just like I'm sure you are right now. After some follow-up questions and a little parental snooping, it turned out the initial reading assessment the student was given took place on a computer with a mouse.

Their son has never used a mouse before and has had very limited access to reading much of anything on a computer. His reading was totally at grade level; it was the assessment that was the problem.

The bigger problem, I'm sure, is that someone, or a committee that someone formed at central office, chose the reading assessment that would be used by teachers. Teachers weren't a part of the conversation because they would have pointed out that their students aren't familiar with using a mouse and that the assessment wouldn't be valid if students had to manipulate the mouse and, simultaneously, concentrate on the assessment.

But nobody did.

You know what would have been a super easy and free thing for those leaders and decision-makers to do? Go visit the classrooms, ask questions about current reading assessments, what technology is available, the ability level of the students with the technology, and then make a decision.

Organizations and those in leadership cannot implement programs without first talking to the people who are going to implement those programs. It just won't work. Being present in classrooms on a daily basis is, for all leadership across an organization, vital in making a plan built for the success of the students.

RAE SAYS

I understand administrative leadership to be a balancing act between two key pieces—a supportive stance and a student-driven mindset.

Now, no one said this was easy to accomplish, but the reality is, the job wasn't built for those with a weak stomach. Having worked for a number of administrative leaders, I know the culture can drastically change depending on the leadership's commitment to being in classrooms.

Last week I was conferencing with four students at a rolling whiteboard over a formative assessment. Looking around the room at the other twenty-eight students working on their personalized projects, I noticed a new face had joined a group sitting on the floor.

I didn't even see him come in! Oops!

With all five of them sitting crisscross applesauce on the carpet, my principal was engaging with students as they explained their mathematical thinking on expressions.

Laughter filled the room as they giggled through the concepts.

No one is perfect, but to me, taking a supportive stance as an administrator means being approachable, open-minded, and relational. You essentially need to ensure you can build systems and relationships at the same time.

As my friend Jeff Gargas would say, you need to build the airplane while in the air. The more we can take this approach while engaging with teachers in real-time, the more effectively we can support those we serve, our students.

As leadership creates plans to enhance our school systems, communicating about them means more than laying out all the facts on a yellow notepad. It's greater than seeing the larger picture of a budget crisis or staffing concerns. It's far more vast than making the choice to be considered "innovative."

It's a dedication to building a plan and then having hundreds of conversations with your teachers around how to build this dream into your school's reality. You can't know where you need to go unless you know where you are. And teachers can't know where to go unless they have the plan in their hands. When staff members can see all those dots, connect them, and see the larger vision—the picture becomes so much clearer.

ADAM SAYS

Thankfully I've always been good at gathering intelligence, and in my daily conversations with our office staff, the principal, or anyone at central office, I was able to piece together some semblance of what may be coming next.

Our office manager had been down at central office for a meeting and heard something about a new district-wide technology initiative that was coming together. That small piece of information, along with the fact that our director of technology had just been to my classroom the week before asking all sorts of questions about iPads and students and curriculum and the network, signaled to me that something must be going on.

Again, it just never made sense to me that the teachers, more often than not, never actually knew what was in the works. Just tell teachers what you're thinking; it's going to be easier and more efficient in the long term and the short term.

If you tell teachers what you're thinking, if you tell teachers what you're planning, if you tell teachers what's on the horizon, you know what happens?

They prepare.

They give you feedback.

They pull from their direct experience working with kids in class-rooms on a daily basis and will be super honest with you about what will work and what needs further discussion.

ADAM SAYS

I knew when I had the opportunity to lead my own school as principal it was going to be different. I was going to be open and honest with all staff, students, and stakeholders in the community about what was on my mind, where we were headed, and how we were going to get there.

I can remember our first school-wide parent meeting and all the looks that were going around. At first I wasn't sure what was going on, so I just asked.

"Is everything okay? People are looking around, and I'm sensing there are questions from the group."

"We've just never gotten this much information before from our principal," someone told me.

It was then that I knew. Inform people, tell them what you're thinking, include them in the decision-making process, and you'll be able to go so much farther, so much faster than you would if you kept it all to yourself.

It's my firm belief that all principals and district office leaders should have a leadership group to meet with and bounce ideas off of. This is where you can get additional feedback, improve your ideas, and keep your finger on the pulse of what's happening and what people are thinking, and then you can move forward with an idea.

Don't shock and awe your teachers—that approach does not work.

You know what it's called when you listen and then tell your teachers and community what the plan is? Caring.

WHAT LEADERS CAN DO

Dear Leaders,

As we mentioned earlier, one of the worst things you can do is shock and awe your staff and community. We don't think too many shock-and-awe campaigns have ever been too successful throughout history, in pretty much any industry.

Maybe you have an idea for a new bell schedule that's going to change the flow of how kids are dropped off in the morning and who goes to lunch and recess at certain times. *And* your kindergarten team is going from a half-day to a full-day program starting next year.

What you shouldn't do is make all the changes yourself and hand everyone the new schedule and say, "This is what we're going to do."

Don't do that.

The first person you should talk with is your custodian. During lunch one day in a casual conversation tell them your idea about changing lunch times and how the flow of recess and lunch will change. If they don't give some ideas right then and there, they'll definitely think on it and get back to you with potential problems that you'll need to massage before it potentially comes to fruition.

Talk with your head office secretary who has been around the school the longest. There's a small to medium chance someone before you had a similar idea. They're going to give you the backstory on what happened and some more variables to think about.

And of course, talk with teachers.

These conversations have to be even more strategic than the previous ones.

Think about your teachers who don't handle change very easily. The ones who've taught multiple grade levels and have experienced different ages and pattern flows throughout the school.

Leadership should be proactive and not defensive, and should get out in front of new ideas and potential issues before they get bigger than you can control. If after a couple of small conversations with key people it really looks like this new idea is going to be way too challenging to get off the ground, you'll probably want to abandon the idea and go back to the drawing board or go after something with far fewer moving parts.

But if those first few conversations show some positive nuggets and seem to have some merit with people, then you keep them up with others on campus (don't forget talking with students also), and then, when you're feeling pretty darn confident, bring your ideas to your entire staff.

There's a difference between not telling people the plan and telling a few people the plan. Because you know what happens when you start telling a few people the plan. They tell others what you told them, which is exactly what you want to happen. Your idea being delivered to someone else by someone other than you is a great strategy! Especially if the person you told first thinks it's a good idea, they're going to help you convince the person they're talking with that the idea has merit without you having to do it yourself.

So in essence you've accomplished a couple things here. You started spreading your idea so teachers know what the plan is, and you're building trust with your organization. Telling a few people your idea before telling everyone at once your idea is usually a good idea.

WHAT TEACHERS CAN DO

Other than your grade level or department team, your students and room parents are key people to keep in the loop of your plans and ideas. It's time to ask for their help.

ADAM SAYS

I really and truly believe we don't give our kids enough credit for what they know, what they can do, how they can help, and the resources they can provide. We don't know until we ask.

When I was a classroom teacher, there was a very sad-looking and dilapidated garden at our school. After years of neglect it became known as "the pit."

One day during recess duty I walked over and decided something needed to be done. The recess bell rang. All the classes went back to their rooms, except us. I brought my students to the fence directly facing the garden and told them, "This is our school's garden; it needs help and we're going to fix it."

We went directly back to class, and everyone was given a piece of large scrap paper to start designing what we wanted the space to look like. Then as a class we started a rather large list on the board of what we'd need in order to restore the garden to its original glory.

The amazing thing was, my students didn't even need me. They made lists of materials we would need. Some went to the computer lab (this was before laptop carts) and printed off pictures of other school gardens to bring back and use for ideas. And something completely miraculous happened—they started adding names to the list of needed supplies, noting who could bring what in from home.

One parent owned a tree company and could surely drop off wood chips for us to use. Another parent was a chef and had some small connection to Alice Waters and her Chez Panisse garden initiative that was happening in a nearby school district.

This went on and on for the next two hours, and I completely let them go with this new project.

You know what they were doing simply because I let them know what the plan was?

They were leading.

They were problem-solving.

They were collaborating.

They were using math concepts when plotting out different areas of the garden and how large some boxes and planters needed to be.

They were thinking strategically about how we could scrounge and gather the necessary items for this new project.

Maybe some of you are thinking, *How does this pertain to* Teachers Deserve It?

Because teachers deserve to not do all the work, we just need to give up control at times in order for the students and teachers and staff to be empowered. Teachers also teach students how to be good leaders, and one way they do that is by modeling good leadership.

And it's all because you told them the plan.

Empower your people.

Share with each other.

Trust that the job is in great hands and is going to get done.

Do not be afraid to ask for help if you don't know how to do something.

It's time for leaders to let their teachers know more of the plan, and it's time for teachers to let go of some responsibility and empower students to take some additional leadership opportunities.

TEACHERS DESERVE GOOD LEADERS

RAE SAYS

I was listening to a podcast once that focused on talking about the absurdities within education. The comedian went on and on by overdramatizing the truths of education and the struggle of being a student.

While I cannot remember the podcast, nor have I heard it in quite some time, one of his lines stuck with me: "Okay, think about it. Teaching is the only job where being promoted means you are not a teacher anymore. You just become a principal or a superintendent."

At the time, I giggled at this, finding humor in the truth I saw in the idea. So many of us enter into the world of education to serve our students, to change lives, and to coach the leaders of tomorrow each and every day.

But truthfully, I hate the statement now because of the major element the comedian missed. Our leaders are still teachers. They went to the same undergraduate programs we all attended. They struggled with the same students we all found challenging. They, too, planned lessons that failed, and they, too, took work home with them at night.

And when they transitioned into leadership roles, their learners changed as well. Now, their learners are us, teachers. Many of our leaders enter into the world of educational leadership to serve their learners, to change lives, and to coach the leaders of tomorrow each and every day. Sound familiar?

The reality is, we understand that being a leader in a building crafted to support students' needs is not an easy position. However, we cannot silence our hopes and aspirations for a leader simply because of the strains and realities of the position.

Why? Because teachers don't do that to themselves. We don't accept excuses. We are solution explorers!

So what type of leaders do teachers deserve?

Erin Hall

High School English Teacher
Rhode Island

I teach to change the future.

I chose to study education in college because I saw how dramatically methods of communication were changing in my own adolescence and wanted to teach people how to be successful communicators in every circumstance, and in every medium. In my classroom, I seek opportunities for students to showcase their mastery of content and connect that mastery to their own lives and interests, in any way that they feel confident. This has resulted in my freshmen running between my classroom and the art lab to use the kiln to create model memorials for World War II heroes, my sophomores waxing poetic into GarageBand for the first time to create the next greatest musical hit, to impromptu debates over Atticus Finch's supposed "sainthood" in the light of the #MeToo era. It is chaotic, creative, collaborative, and I absolutely love every minute of it!

I also model progressive innovation for my students by constantly trying out the latest best practice in blended or personalized learning and remaining transparent with my students about how we both feel it is going. That authentic communication shows my students that the concept of "growth mindset" doesn't go away after graduation. It is my way of reflecting the future that my students will find outside of my classroom, while still creating a safe space for experimentation, exploration, and general enjoyment of learning.

I know that my students are going to create the reality of their wildest dreams, and those dreams will set the world on fire. That is why I teach.

THE LIST

Teachers deserve a leader:

- That will stand in front of them, next to them, or beside them—depending on the situation.
- That will have their back in public and, if needed, coach them in private.
- That will appreciate the rigors of their job and support them however they can.
- That will show up, every single day, with a smile on their face.
- That will substitute teach in their classroom when the school is short on subs.
- That doesn't forget how fun it is to be a teacher and also how completely challenging it can be on a daily basis.
- That knows it's more complicated, more demanding, more strenuous, more program heavy, more trauma informed, and just so much more than when they were still in the classroom.
- That will visit their classroom on a weekly basis to spend time, check in, build relationships with students, and know the pulse of what's going on at the school so they can be a better support system when it's needed.
- That doesn't just come into a classroom twice a year every few years to do their evaluation, because that's not a fair representation of what happens day in and day out there.
- That remembers everyone has a bad day now and then.
- That knows the work teachers do at school is so important, but that a teacher's family is more important and comes first.
- That may not know everything, but who's going to help solve the issue and get teachers the help, support, materials, or relief they need to do their job.
- That doesn't schedule meetings just to schedule meetings, just because they were supposed to schedule a meeting.

- That values teachers' time, education, experience, inspiration, family, strengths, areas for growth, health, and ideas when it comes to shared decision making.
- That treats them like professionals, period.
- That will still teach a class from time to time, if it's an hour, half a day, or all day—so they don't forget what it's like, because the longer you're out of the classroom, the more you're going to forget.
- That will use assessment data and standardized test scores in a planning conversation, but not as a way to discipline teachers for not doing their jobs.
- That treats teachers like human beings, because they are.
- That will give open, honest, constructive, and well-thought-out feedback because they want them to get better as an educator, and not because they "messed up."
- That lets them wear jeans to school without having to earn a free pass or pay money for it.
- That knows the contract and respects the collective bargaining agreement.
- That can admit when they make a mistake, because everyone makes mistakes.
- That knows the curriculum, because if they don't, how will they support a teacher and have conversations about their classroom?
- That will advocate for teachers—with parents, central office, elected officials, colleagues, and anyone else that tries to teacher-shame someone on their team.
- That will congratulate teachers when they do something great, face-to-face and in front of peers, because it's really important that teachers are celebrated.
- That takes a genuine interest in the parent community, building relationships and creating a welcoming environment so everyone feels welcome and heard.
- That asks those tough questions, because those are the questions that need to be asked in order to learn and grow together. If it's all

rainbows and frozen yogurt, they're probably not asking the right questions and having the real conversations.

- That enjoys coming to work every day, because if they don't, that vibe will permeate throughout the school and not be good for anyone.

RAE SAYS

So, who are our leaders? When originally crafting the idea for a leadership chapter with Adam, I immediately thought about administration.

What type of principal do teachers deserve?

What type of curriculum director do teachers deserve?

What type of superintendents do teachers deserve?

And, like you saw above, Adam and I created quite a list.

But then an early morning phone call with a colleague challenged my thinking.

As we talk about the leadership a teacher deserves, is administration the only responsible party for these attributes?

Leadership within a progressive school building is so much more than a title and generous paycheck. Leadership is more than administrators. Leadership must be something that teachers show, too. Leaders take many forms:

- Teacher leaders
- Mentors
- Coaches
- Instructional support
- Department chairs
- Students
- Paraprofessionals
- Your parent community

Frankly, anyone who is in any sort of role model position to other human beings has a responsibility to uphold the elements of a good leader.

Teachers deserve a principal who can admit that they may not know everything and who's going to help solve the issue and get you the support, materials, or relief that you need to do your job. Teachers also deserve instructional coaches and colleagues who can do this as well.

Teachers deserve a principal who doesn't schedule meetings just to schedule meetings, just because they were supposed to schedule a meeting. They also deserve PBIS coaches and tech coaches who do the same.

Teachers deserve a principal who values their time, education, experience, inspiration, family, strengths, areas for growth, health, and ideas when it comes to shared decision making. Teachers also deserve mentors and teacher leaders who respect the same.

We must set a new leadership standard for the entire ecosystem that aims to support teachers in the trenches. We must all hold ourselves a little higher as we work to be role models for the students we serve.

THE SOLUTION

Yikes! Did you really think you'd find a way to achieve everything on this list here? If we were that good, we'd be flying around in a helicopter made of gold and live in a beautiful house with fifteen rescue dogs (possibly Rae's dream, not Adam's).

Nevertheless, here are the truths we can provide.

Choosing to be the leader every teacher deserves is a choice. You can beg, barter, and plead for someone to change for the better, but changing is an active choice a leader must make on their own.

Start small. Choose one item from the list above or an area for growth you think up on your own. Begin by just having it in your mind, and then eventually transition into putting a plan into action.

Regardless of how others around you may act, choose to model how a leader should act.

No one said it would be easy—we actually stated in the beginning it wouldn't be—but you can do it.

How do we know? Because you are an educator.

Teachers deserve good leaders, so start by being the leader you had as a teacher, being the role model you had as a student, or simply being the one you wish you had. Lead by example.

TEACHERS DESERVE GOOD COACHES

Like we said before, colleagues are important. Friends are important. Your leader or boss is important.

We think a coach is also really important for teachers, and everyone needs one! Maybe you're wondering what the difference between a coach and a boss is. Let us explain. Your boss (leader) is most definitely and should be a coach. They should encourage you, help you with problem solving, do your evaluation, and hopefully overall make sure you have what you need to do your job. Your boss should give you valuable feedback on your performance and in other areas to help make you as successful as possible.

A coach or mentor is someone who is not your evaluator, they may or may not be a direct colleague, and they most definitely have open and honest conversations about work and how they can best support you to crush it at your job.

ADAM SAYS

In California when I started teaching many years ago, everyone was given a coach for their first two years. It's a pretty formal program that is taken seriously—with rules, timelines, mandatory meetings between the teacher and coach, and a culminating project that incorporates lots of reflection and evidence to support the teacher's growth.

At first I wasn't too sure how to approach my coaching relationship. I'd been a lifelong athlete and on baseball or soccer teams since I was a little boy and had one vision of a "coach" in my brain, and this experience was so much different and so necessary.

The coach that took me under her wing was another teacher at my school, someone with years of experience. They'd attended a coaching clinic and been certified to do this type of work with new teachers, and it was exactly what I needed and, in my opinion, what everyone needs no matter where they are in their career.

A coach is meant to be objective, open, and honest, and to give the right feedback so that you grow as a professional. Every leader is a little bit different, and every coach will have different characteristics as well, but the coach should have a more narrow focus that is completely objective.

Coaches listen without passing judgment on performance because it's meant to be a learning relationship. Sometimes their listening is just that, without any advice or counsel, because everyone needs someone to vent to every now and then.

Be careful with sharing too many work stories with your spouse, significant other, or friends—they're going to get tired of your work stories and someday may end up not even listening at all.

Coaches advise, because they're not giving you a formal evaluation. They're working with you so you can learn and grow as a professional.

RAE SAYS

I have had so many outstanding coaches in my life. And while it has not always been easy, I have always tried to soak up as much knowledge from them as possible.

My first coach evaluated my strengths and weaknesses as an educator in dynamic ways, to collect enough information about me to give me necessary constructive and honest feedback. This coach really saw the learning process as an ART: he was dedicated to Analyzing my needs, forming an authentic Relationship with me built on trust, and providing me Tactical strategies to be my best self.

Fletcher Nelson
Third-Grade Teacher
Minnesota

I'm not one of those people who always knew they wanted to be a teacher. I actually never considered it until my senior year of high school. My guidance counselor suggested I go help out in a fourth-grade classroom during an open hour I had in my schedule. Every day when I arrived, the kids were always so excited to see me! Regardless of how the rest of my day was, that hour of the day always put me in a good mood, and that's when I decided I wanted to be a teacher!

So why do I teach? I do it for the twenty-five high-fives and hugs I get each morning. I do it for the relationships I build with my students throughout the year. I do it for the visits from former students. I do it for the invites to their sporting events and concerts. I do it for the kids!

Maybe you're thinking, *I want a coach, but my district doesn't provide them!*

Well then, you need to go out and find your own. If you are choosing to live solo on Educator Island in 2020, that's totally up to you. But hopefully you've decided to build a worldwide professional learning network (see chapter 8) and have a plethora of fellow educators that could coach you.

It's really important to take the time to develop relationships, and to know others' educational interests and personality types. With all of that being said, there is no formula when choosing a coach that's going to help you along your professional journey. Finding a coach is kind of like dating; if you're looking too hard for one, you probably won't find the right one, but if you're putting yourself out there in a genuine and honest way, then your chances of connecting with the person that's right for you are much higher.

We'd also recommend letting people that are close to you and well connected know what you're looking for. That word-of-mouth connection is so valuable and may just be the catalyst to finding the coach that can push you, ask you, urge you, listen to you, and be there for you.

DOS AND DON'TS

Choose to be active in the coaching process. No one likes a passive participant. See each meeting and conversation as a call to action to improve your practice. Sit up, take notes, and soak it up like a sponge!

Don't take things personally. It's a good sign if you're sometimes caught slightly off guard by your coach. That means they're being honest in their feedback and keeping it real with you so that you get better.

Be patient with your coach and use them when you really think you need them. Don't ask them about every single situation. Be selective.

Keep the relationship completely confidential. We can't stress this enough.

Tell your coach thank you, that you appreciate them, and also thanks for always challenging your ideas and thought process.

Take feedback with a grain of salt. A coach intends to be your mentor and cheerleader. But there's a certain magic only *you* can bring as an educator, so don't lose your sense of self. Reflect on the coaching you receive, and find your own pizzazz in the process.

Coaching is not a punishment. Do not allow yourself to be embarrassed that you are receiving coaching. The truth is, everyone in every profession in every role grows from these same strategies.

Your coach is not your friend. You're in this relationship together to improve. At times they're going to say things you may not want to hear. Don't take it personally, and remember they have your best interest in mind, even if it doesn't seem that way.

Coaching is a gift—share it! Choose to share what you've learned with other colleagues and network members. You can provide so much value to others this way!

#TEACHERSDESERVEIT EDUCATOR EXPERIMENT

It ain't easy to become a good leader, but you can do it!

1. Take one of the leadership attributes listed above and put it into action! Begin by grabbing a clean sheet of paper. Write down a list of leadership attributes you wish to possess. Choose 3–5.

2. Start small. Keep these attributes at the top of your mind for the next month, then put a plan in place to develop them. Snap a picture of yourself working on one of the steps of your plan, and share it using #TeachersDeserveIt.

3. Create your flowchart so you can keep track of the plan! Identify the things you are working on as an educator—whether it's a new initiative or another idea you are working toward improving. Using a

graphic organizer, show how all the pieces fit together to support students. Hang this near your workspace to remind you how your efforts are building the strong foundation for your future success! Share your image using #TeachersDeserveIt for others to see!

4. Give your coach a shout-out! Have you experienced an outstanding mentor in your life so far (maybe even more than one)? It's time to share the love. How did they master the ART of coaching by Analyzing your needs, building a trust-focused Relationship, and providing you Tactical strategies to improve? Send them a quick handwritten note or tag them in a tweet with your appreciation. Use #TeachersDeserveIt to inspire others to do the same on your favorite social media platform!

CHAPTER 6

Teachers Deserve Fair Evaluations

Performing evaluations is a leadership skill, and how a principal handles this process tells you a lot about that person as a leader. But evaluations are also about how teachers are perceived at work, and teachers deserve fair evaluations.

In preparation and during the writing of this book, we sent out questions to our PLN on social media, asking what they feel teachers deserve. The answers have been quite broad, with a few glaring similarities every time we've asked. One similarity that continually popped up is the desire for a fair and diverse evaluation process.

At first we didn't make much of the coincidence, but then, as we talked about our own experiences with evaluations, we realized there was room for improvement and that we needed to write about it.

P. Sloan Joseph

Instructional Technology Coach, Educational Consultant
South Carolina

"This was a week from hell! Mediations, dress code violations, and they always have an excuse about why they are late!" On a cold December evening in 2003, I poured my heart out to my best friend, Ronaele. She laughed and said, "Sounds like you work at my school. You should become a teacher. Since you work with both salaried and hourly employees, you'd be able to prepare students for college and career." I thought, *No, ma'am. I'm working in the HR department of a Fortune 500 company. I have the potential to make six figures one day.*

Ronaele was a respected biology teacher. I was honored that she thought I could influence students to be successful adults. Her words impacted me in ways I didn't expect. I'd been a substitute teacher while attending college. I enjoyed it, but I majored in business administration, not education. One day, I checked the local school district's website. It was January, so I didn't think there would be any business education positions available. There were two high school positions posted! I applied, interviewed, and was offered both positions! Although I didn't have my teaching license, they were willing to give me an opportunity to prove myself.

I accepted a position teaching business, marketing, and computer technology.

Over the years, I've had many successes and failures, laughter and tears. No matter what, I always return to why I started: hope for our future. I hope I show faith in others like my first school showed when hiring me. I hope I've fulfilled the dreams of my parents. They were the first generation to attend college, moving away from family and friends to live in an area that provided better job opportunities and access to quality education. They took risks to make life better for my sisters and me. I hope I never forget to take risks to make things better for students and teachers. For those risks are necessary in preparing our next generation of leaders.

ADAM SAYS

I had the same principal for all of my years as a teacher except one, and if I was being evaluated that year, they only came in twice, during the entire year. One year I can remember their phone ringing during class, and he went outside for twenty minutes to take the call, during my official and scheduled observation—that's just not fair.

It was during that experience, among many others, that I told myself, "If I ever become a principal someday, I'm going to do it much differently."

Teachers deserve a fair and diverse evaluation process, and that means their evaluator needs to spend a lot of time in their classroom when they're not being evaluated so they can see the entire picture, and not just a snapshot lesson that may not always go exactly as planned.

Now, we fully understand each state and individual district has different rules when it comes to evaluations, and we respect that. But we also know that the presence of building principals in classrooms is paramount for a fair and diverse evaluation.

ADAM SAYS

When I did become a principal, I reflected on my past experience from my time in the classroom. My last year teaching, our new principal was in classrooms all the time. I loved it, but many other teachers did not.

She was getting to know the students. Connecting with teachers. Seeing what worked and what needed to be improved. You can't know where your school needs to go unless you know where you are. And you can't know where you are if you're not in classrooms on a daily basis.

My goal as a new leader was to be in every classroom every day for the first hundred days of school. At first there was some grumbling among the teachers.

"What does he want?"

"Why is he in classrooms so much?"

"Jane [the former principal] hasn't been in my room for years. Why is he checking up on us?"

Hasn't been in a classroom for *years*? How can your administrator give you a fair and diverse evaluation when they only see snippets of you teaching? It just doesn't make sense.

Being in classrooms is not about checking up on teachers, it's about seeing the big picture. It's about observing those small moments that happen every single day that can and should be celebrated with students and teachers.

It's about the leader scheduling and conducting the formal observations that go into a teacher's file, and knowing that those are only snapshots of the bigger picture. The small daily moments help the leader understand, develop, and justify those formal observations when they go as planned—and more importantly when they don't go as planned.

RAE SAYS

When I was learning about the evaluation process as a new teacher, I was introduced to a model that asked me to use a rubric and put forth a great deal of effort to provide evidence of the work I was doing.

In some capacity, I really like that I was given a voice and choice in this evaluation system. I enjoyed looking through the rubric and noting the work I was doing in those areas. But *gosh*, did it take a long time! I spent hours on Saturday mornings and Sunday afternoons for weeks reading through the rubric, hoping to identify three to five pieces of evidence for the more than thirty-two sections of the evaluation.

The process was tedious. Honestly, it felt like I was back to working on my master's—hunched over piles of papers, annotating and highlighting text to evaluate its meaning and put it into my own words to construct an argument.

I wondered, if my leadership was more active in understanding the goings-on of the day-to-day routine of my classroom and the "why" behind my instruction, would I feel the need to add so much detail to my evidence bank? Or was it their lack of knowledge that caused me to feel the stress on my shoulders to prove my worth to them each year?

When leaders are present every single day in classrooms, and then they conduct the formal observation, they know all the pieces to the puzzle and they can help the teacher put them together. If you don't have all the pieces, you're not going to be able to finish the puzzle. It's somewhat like doing a Sudoku puzzle. If you have to guess when doing a Sudoku, you really shouldn't write the number down, because it's a lot less likely to help you solve the puzzle.

A teacher observation is similar. Don't go into that classroom without all the information you need to contextualize what you observe.

ADAM SAYS

Something funny happened when, after the first hundred days or so, I eased off of being in every classroom every day. If I missed a day or two of visiting, teachers would come and find me. Students would seek me out on the playground or at lunch: "Mr. Welcome, where have you been? We haven't seen you in our classrooms in so long."

It had only been one or two days, but it's then that I realized the habit had made a difference. Teachers and students appreciated my presence. Building relationships. The conversations that happen when the leader is a part of the teaching and learning.

And for me, it made the "formal" evaluation process so much easier and more fun to be a part of. If the formal observation didn't totally go as planned, it didn't really matter. Because I'd already seen dozens if not hundreds of other lessons that the teacher had knocked out of the park. And I would write up that formal observation as a summary of the bigger picture, because that's what teachers deserve, and that's real life.

If a student was acting out in class and not fully accessing the curriculum, it didn't matter as much because I already knew that may happen from my previous time in class, which also allowed us to find the proper strategies to best support the teacher and the student.

When leaders develop a culture of visibility and implement a fair and diverse evaluation process, teachers feel more relaxed.

They are more themselves.

They smile more.

They take risks they may not have in the past.

They have more open and honest conversations with their evaluator because they know that they can.

They stop doubting themselves so much and focus on their strengths.

They let go of some control during the lesson because they know the formal evaluation isn't punitive, it's one snapshot of the bigger picture.

Evaluations are important. There is no denying evaluations are a part of our work that needs to stay. However, the process needs some flexibility, some broader understanding, some additional time in classrooms when things aren't as formal, some patience when a lesson goes sideways, some real relationships so the evaluator and the evaluatee can work together and not against each other, because they are on the same team.

Let's all work together better to evaluate the full educator, just like we are all dedicated to teaching the full child!

#TEACHERSDESERVEIT
EDUCATOR EXPERIMENT

It's time for you to allow your evaluator to know more about what goes on inside your classroom! Reach out to the principal this week and invite them in!

1. Don't put on a show or plan a special activity for the visit. Just be you! Then, follow up with a quick conversation. Pop into their office or catch them in the hallway.

2. What do you talk about in your follow up conversation? Simply how much you appreciate them seeing X while in your classroom because it is something you are really passionate about! And then—invite them in again!

Nicole Marte

Middle School Science Teacher
Georgia

When I was younger, I would set my stuffed animals up, use the old projector we had, and teach them different lessons. I thought I wanted to be a teacher, until I got older. It seemed like my passion for teaching left when I was in middle and high school. I would've said you were crazy if you told me I would become a teacher.

My major was undecided for my first two years in college. I really had no idea or direction for my career. After a long talk with my husband, I realized that whatever I decided to do had to involve helping people. I ended up getting my degree in psychology because I thought I wanted to be a counselor. I was then hired as an administrative assistant in a counseling office and realized that I didn't enjoy office jobs. We were living in Florida, and then my husband received a job in Georgia. When we arrived in Georgia, I had to find a job for myself. One of my friends suggested that I start subbing in the schools.

I was hesitant at first because I remembered how substitutes were treated when I was in school, but I decided to give it a shot. I started subbing in various schools and quickly fell in love. My heart was with the middle school students, and I dreamed of having a classroom of my own one day. Long story short, I completed the testing necessary to receive a teaching job and got hired as a sixth-grade science teacher. It's so ironic that I'm a science teacher now because I struggled in science when I was in school. I felt like it was a lot of textbook work and not a lot of hands-on activities. This drives me to make science exciting and engaging. My favorite is when students write me notes or tell me that they never liked science until they had me. Science is made to be intriguing, and I love introducing my students to the wonders of science!

When I tell people I'm a middle school teacher, I usually get one of a few responses: "Oh, bless your heart!" "I don't know how you do it!"

or "That's a tough age!" If I'm being honest, I get it. Most people had less than appealing middle school experiences, and students are at the age where they are figuring out who they are. However, this is the perfect age for me. They are old enough to be independent and understand jokes but young enough to still be impressionable and want a relationship with their teacher.

Teaching middle school is never boring! Their randomness keeps me entertained and laughing every day. It also helps to have amazing co-workers and teammates who can laugh at their randomness with you. My teammates have helped me through really difficult times in my teaching career, and I'm so thankful for them. They really make the bad times bearable and the good times even better.

When I think about why I teach, my "why" has always been the students. I believe teachers should be passionate not only about the content but also about who the individual student is outside the classroom. The saying "A child doesn't care how much you know until they know how much you care" has guided me through my teaching journey. When kids know you care (and they know when it's real), you become more than just a teacher of content. You become a teacher of friendships, relationships, respect, and kindness (just to name a few).

When a student shares an impact I've made in their life, it means the world to me. It's priceless. I keep all handwritten notes, gifts, and pictures in a box in my room to remind me of my "why" on difficult days. I remember a note given to me on the last day of school from one of my students, and it said, "The only reason I would wake up in the morning was to come see you and be in your class." Teaching can be so discouraging at times, but it's moments and notes like this that make it all worth it.

I can't save them from their hard times, but I can be a voice of guidance and hope. These students are our future, and I feel so honored that I get to play a small part in their growth and ultimately their life. I honestly can't see myself in any other profession. My students have been and always will be my "why."

CHAPTER 7

Teachers Deserve Higher Pay and Smaller Class Sizes

What do teachers and collective bargaining groups usually always ask for? Higher pay and lower class size. The #RedForEd movement has grown exponentially over the past few years, and we think teachers using their voice and advocating for both ideas is so vitally important. We don't know when some type of lasting change will happen, but we can educate others about what we're up against and why change is needed.

There's really no other way to say this—teachers deserve higher pay.

ADAM SAYS

When I was a twenty-two-year-old brand-new teacher, I didn't just teach. I tutored two days a week after school for a few hours. I also worked at a running shoe store every Saturday and Sunday from 11:30 to 7:30 for the first seven years I worked in public education.

Now don't get me wrong, I kind of knew what I was getting myself into. My dad was a public school teacher for thirty-five years, and there was always the saying "You don't get into teaching for the money."

I get that, but something needs to change in a profound way.

People get into other professions because of the money they'll earn. Why should education be any different? I want to make a difference in the lives of children and get paid really well. There's nothing at all wrong with that. Financial stress preoccupies the mind in a major way, and I wonder how many teachers are negatively affected by this.

It's now been almost twenty years since I got that first teaching job, and looking back on my seven-day work week, I feel some anger. I'm angry that I had to work two other part-time jobs in order to pay my monthly student loans, rent, car payment, and other bills, and to try to save any little bit of money that I could.

And let me tell you, I do not have expensive taste. My car payment was going toward a stripped-down Ford Ranger pickup, a very basic one-bedroom apartment, student loans from a private college that I now wish I hadn't gone to. Whatever was left over went to going out with friends and my savings account. I didn't have a cell phone bill back then, because cell phones didn't exist. I wasn't buying an Apple Watch, because it didn't exist. You can always spend money on something, but I wasn't—because there just wasn't enough to go around on my salary as a teacher.

Rae and I both have the opportunity to travel the country and meet educators from many different states. Wherever I go, it's the same conversation.

Teachers driving for Uber or Lyft at night and on the weekends to help pay their bills or to save money for a house.

Teachers tutoring after school and on the weekends and teaching summer school or being a camp counselor when school is out for the year.

Teachers living with their parents to help save money.

Teachers living with three or four roommates because rent is just too expensive.

The San Francisco Unified School District has actually started building their own housing for teachers because they have such a hard time with recruitment. Here's why: The average price of a one-bedroom apartment in San Francisco is $3,600 a month. The starting salary for a new teacher in SFUSD is $57,000. That means 73 percent of a teacher's salary in San Francisco goes to their rent if they live in the city where they work. Unless you have no car payment, no student loans, and no credit card payments, you're going to have very little money left over to do much of anything after your rent is paid, starting with buying groceries.

Some people may feel this is a district problem. School districts are given funds from their state, and they along with school boards decide where to spend money, how much to pay teachers, etc. We say the problem is much bigger than that. The problem can only be addressed by making teacher pay a priority across our entire country, at a state and federal level.

ACTION STEPS

The issue of teacher pay is real. And it's inhibiting amazing young people from getting into the profession, or even staying in the profession because the pay just isn't enough.

We need to share our stories. Please share *your* story and force others to see the problem firsthand. Any one of the actions below could be taken by you today.

- Share your "why" for becoming an educator with your friends and family
- Write a letter to your governor
- Send one note to a congressperson
- Reach out to a state senator
- Craft a message to the secretary of education
- Share your story by attending a school board meeting
- Go on a free website right now and write blog posts
- Consider future employment with a district that supports continued education for movement on the pay scale

- Make a three-minute video to post on YouTube so that community members, politicians, and non-educators can hear your message
- And most importantly, don't give up. Fight for what you need— for what all teachers need.

Everyone makes personal choices about how they spend their money—that's no secret. But teachers should not have to worry about paying bills, buying food, or missing a student loan payment because their chosen profession just doesn't pay enough money to make ends meet. Fight for higher pay so you can pay your bills. Go on a vacation. Buy a new car when yours is run down and needs repair. Take your significant other out to dinner and an evening away.

None of the steps in this book are easy, and change is always incremental. The truth is, if change was easy and instantaneous, teachers would not be in the position they are now. Teacher pay has been a problem. It continues to be a problem. And we must do something, because we can do better for our teachers.

TEACHERS ALSO DESERVE SMALLER CLASS SIZES

Large class sizes are detrimental for our students. When teachers wear red and picket about large class sizes, let's be clear: teachers aren't casting themselves in the role of "victim." They're doing what they do best: fighting for what kids deserve and making their voices heard so that our students can get the support they need to learn and grow.

RAE SAYS

I will never forget when my eighth-hour science class had thirty-eight sixth graders on the roster. I have vivid memories of looking at my student list and thinking, *Gosh, I hope that's a typo.*

In a building with high mobility and where students being pulled out for intervention from their science class was common practice, I assumed the body count of thirty-eight was an error. No way was my classroom, where it was already a struggle to navigate around with the bulky desks blocking you in every direction, going to include that number of learners.

I looked around the room and began counting the desks: "One, two, three . . . thirty-three, thirty-four. Ugh, I don't even have enough desks!"

How was I going to fit four more seats in here? Could students sit on the floor? Or maybe the edge of the window?

I had already eliminated my teacher desk when my student class size increased from thirty to thirty-four. What was left to take out of the room to make space?

Well, who needs seats anyway? I thought.

To be honest, I think the biggest struggle for me was centered around managing thirty-eight students' needs day in, day out.

Is classroom management a struggle? Sure.

Is it difficult to build strong relationships with that number of students quickly? Sure.

Does it mean more copies and more grading? Sure.

But the major concern I had was centered around what came after all those details. When all of those areas were taken care of. When students respected their learning environment and became a family in our classroom. After I learned the students' names, hobbies, and what made them tick. After I had the copies made. My concern centered around not wanting the number of students in my classroom to dictate my ability to help them learn and not slip through the cracks.

No matter your class size, every student is on their individual journey toward better learning. If you have twenty young minds, you have twenty different needs. If you have forty students, you need forty different strategic supports.

How do we expect teachers to support each and every one of these areas each and every day of the school year?

Gosh, and we wonder why teacher burnout is on the rise?

Dennis Griffin

Elementary Principal
Wisconsin

Teachers deserve a culture of collaboration and support. This means moving from a "do as you are told" mentality to a mindset of "we are partners." Focusing on your title and thinking, *This is not my job* is a sure way to derail a school culture and erode a culture of collaboration.

A few years ago, we were experiencing a teacher shortage a couple of months into the school year. As a leader, this was a challenge for me. What was more challenging was watching one of the new hires begin to doubt her abilities because she didn't know who her partner would be from one day to the next. The school community was beginning to ask questions as well. This only added to the pressure on me but more importantly it was straining the culture of our school.

One Friday, I went to the new educator and said, "Can we talk for a second?" She began to cry and said that she was feeling the weight of the world and didn't want others to judge her based on what was currently happening. I said, "You do not have to cry about that anymore. As a matter of fact, I have a crazy idea . . . I will be your partner until we can find you a permanent one." Honestly, I think this made her cry a little more. I think she was waiting for me to say that this was a joke. I shared with her that I did not have all of the logistics ironed out, but Monday we would make the shift.

News spread quickly about the plan, and there were many questions that came up regarding how this was going to happen. Honestly, there were several administrative friends of mine that told me that this was a bad idea. They said my job was to be the principal of the school and not the teacher. To a certain degree, they were correct. However, one of the most important responsibilities that I have is to help create and protect our school culture. I also knew that this was a great opportunity to model a culture of collaboration. Slowly but surely every educator in the building made their way past the room when I was teaching. I always asked them for feedback. My partner and I began to collaborate on combining our classes to cross integrate the lessons. I remember that we used Dr. Seuss's *The Cat in the Hat* and a gravity lesson with stacking cups. I was a teacher during the day for one month. My partner helped me with the planning and creation of many of the anchor charts for my room as I tried to create a balance between my roles.

I remember talking with her one day as our time as teaching partners was coming to a close, and she said that I was very different and she understood why her friend spoke so highly of me. I told her that I didn't do anything special or out of the ordinary. All I did was support her, and that was the only thing that mattered because I valued her as a member of our school community. She shared with me that she enjoyed the experience and that many of the educators asked her how it was collaborating with the principal. She said at first it was a little challenging and weird. For example, she said, "If he messed up, I was reluctant to say anything because he was the evaluator. However, he wanted the feedback." Then it just became natural. She said she didn't even view me as just the principal anymore. She viewed me as her partner. That was the highest compliment that could have been afforded to me during that time. It is a time that I will never forget. The thing is, to this day we still acknowledge each other as teaching partners.

Far too often, educators have not experienced the power of being on a great team. We think that it happens in passing. I believe that every teacher should be supported by administrators and one another to ensure they are part of a strong collaborative team that will enhance the culture and the learning opportunities of the school.

EXPERIENCE MATTERS

Personal experience is important in relation to class size. When you've experienced teaching both larger classes and smaller ones, it all really makes more sense.

ADAM SAYS

My first few years as a teacher in California were in fifth grade. Most teachers in my district had thirty to thirty-two students in class, and boy were those kids packed in tight. Larger desks, larger kids, and starting in April, after lunch you could smell them more, too—the deodorant conversation was always a fun one.

Looking back on those first few years, I have so many fond memories of great projects we worked on in class, fun times and jokes we would play to keep the learning fun, and it's the students from those first few years in my early twenties that I have the most trouble remembering.

We had fun.

We got through the curriculum.

We went to fifth-grade outdoor camp.

We sent them all off to middle school.

We did all those report cards.

Had all of those conferences twice a year.

It's just a challenge to remember their names and specific interactions I had.

Fast-forward to the end of my third year, and there was an opening in third grade.

I jumped at the chance to try a different grade level with a new team of teachers and, of course, a class-size reduction. I moved rooms over the summer and had to go back with a tape measure to my old one. Was this new room bigger? Even though it was part of the same brand-new school? Nope, I had twelve fewer desks because class size capped at twenty in the lower grades. My new room felt empty.

There is research out there with data that says a smaller class size doesn't improve instruction or access to the curriculum. And what I would say is that research and data don't tell the whole story.

Research and data don't measure relationships. They don't measure having to give more assessments, complete more report cards, have that many more conferences. They don't measure the ability to get to know all of your students.

My time teaching third grade is so much more memorable. Is it because I was a more experienced teacher and felt more comfortable in the classroom? Maybe a little. But I can remember the students in those classes so much more than I can those first few years in fifth grade.

I had more time to build relationships.

To go deeper with projects and push each individual learner to new heights.

Parent conferences went longer and more in depth because I wasn't worried about cramming them all into a few days, because I had fewer of them to have to prepare for and complete.

Simply put, there was less stress, less anxiety, less fear that I wasn't going to have the time to connect with each child on their learning.

We had more time, because we had fewer students.

Smaller classes work. They're not convenient when districts have budget problems. And politicians will cite evidence and data that they don't make a difference, even though those same people have never taught a day in their lives. It's the human data that you can't measure on a test that makes a real difference, and that difference is the most important of all.

PERSONALIZATION TO MEET NEEDS

Real talk: Teacher class size needs to be fixed nationwide. And when the going gets tough, this cannot be the first area that goes for the sake of a budget. If we want good education, we need manageable class sizes and prepared educators to get us there.

So, what do we do now? Before the policies change. Before the lawmakers schedule their session to discuss this issue. Before the money is granted. Do we simply ask educators to keep treading water and tell them a solution is coming . . . someday?

Nah. Educators are no longer "sit back and wait" kind of people.

Structure can be a huge part of supporting our need to build authentic relationships with students and add a personalized instructional environment to support all of our learners.

As students explore, question, converse, and reflect, a teacher's role is to facilitate learning. This is a massive shift in the educational community over the last two decades. And, in many cases, this shift is challenging for teachers to make because many have not seen it successfully modeled for them.

Leadership: "Hey! You've spent twenty-two years as a student in the education system and now ten years as an educator, but we need you to start teaching completely differently now due to the Google-, YouTube-, and Netflix-obsessed students entering into your classrooms. Jobs are changing so classrooms must, too. Think you can have that ready by next week?"

Well, joke's on them, friends! We can adapt. Why? Because we are teachers.

We are dedicated to our craft and committed to our students' best interests. If that means I need to learn a new dance move, try out a new tech tool, and overhaul all that I thought I knew about education—fine. #KidsDeserveIt.

But even with the best of intentions, some tips and tricks on effective ways to implement new strategies are always appreciated. You need a framework to operate in and a network of support to brainstorm with.

Kevin Butler

Fifth-Grade Teacher and Director of K–6 Curriculum and Instruction
California

Every morning my students write in their journals. They are asked to answer two questions. The first is always: "How do you feel today and why?" Several years ago, after my class was dismissed, a student left his journal open on top of his desk. While I try not to make a habit of reading students' entries, it was obvious to me the student wanted me to read it. He wrote how much he felt valued as a member of the class, and for the first time, he looked forward to coming to school. He went on to thank me for believing in him, and he knew that I was helping him become a better person.

Moments like these are the reason I am a teacher. Every day, I go to work and have the privilege to be a part of something bigger. The human connection between teachers and their students is powerful. Without a doubt, I have the best job in the world. I love being a teacher, and quite honestly, I could not imagine doing anything else.

Regardless of the framework you choose, the best way to support students who are falling through the cracks is to adopt a mastery learning mindset coupled with a personalized learning approach toward instruction. Find the right way to implement it into your classroom routines.

In the simplest of terms, *mastery learning* is focused on students having the time to achieve a full understanding in an area prior to moving forward to more challenging content. *Personalized learning* allows the student to have voice and choice throughout their learning. When you put these together, you can create rich experiences for students that truly focus on the act of learning over task completion.

RAE SAYS

When I started exploring bringing mastery learning with a personalized learning approach into my classroom, I was skeptical. I vividly remember being on a Google Hangout call with Chad Ostrowski, a former middle school teacher and the CEO of the Teach Better Team. He was talking on and on about how, even in a room full of different student needs, he was able to conference with students daily and see growth across the board in his classroom.

It wasn't that I thought he was lying to me. I just didn't see how this idea would work for me in my classroom. My students were in a rural setting. His were in an urban setting. He was at a large school. I was in a small school. He had little parent involvement. I had active parent involvement. We just seemed to be worlds apart.

I think I actually told him, "I love the idea of mastery learning, but I don't believe it is possible in a public school classroom."

I am giggling right now writing this for all of you, because I later discovered how wrong I was, and it completely changed me as an educator.

I don't want to get on my soapbox, because I really could talk forever on this topic, my transformation as a classroom teacher, and how my students thrived—I mean, the data was like night and day—but it's not about my students.

This is about you and your choice to do what is right to reach your learners.

Regardless of the pathway you choose to explore to personalizing student learning in your classroom, this initiative will drastically affect the students you are able to reach in a given class hour.

Think about it: if you can provide the students the support they need exactly when they need it each and every day—and then allow them to thrive and work collaboratively the rest of the time, you'll have built a sustainable classroom environment dedicated to growth regardless of the roster number.

You *can* do it. Let's adopt a growth mindset like the one we challenge our learners to have every day and rise up to the challenge.

#TEACHERSDESERVEIT EDUCATOR EXPERIMENT

Choose one action from the list about advocating for higher teacher pay and do it today. Ready, set, go! Share your plans using #TeachersDeserveIt for others to see!

1. What strategy do you use in your classroom to reach as many of your students as possible? Share out your favorite tool or strategy using #TeachersDeserveIt for others to learn more about this idea. Every problem teachers have in their classrooms has a solution that exists in another classroom around the world—we just need to find it! Help be the solution for others!

CHAPTER 8

Teachers Deserve to Be Connected

Choosing to live on your own teacher island may *sound* appealing. However, if you've ever truly experienced an isolated state, one with little to no contact with others, you might understand why many people struggle.

We are social creatures, and surrounding ourselves with people we love is essential to our development, perspective, and growth. However, we often find educators choose to isolate themselves professionally. A community or network matters. Other people can provide support and help solve problems. Other people provide shoulders to cry on, shoulders to stand on, listening ears to vent to, and the solution-seeking brains we crave.

There are two avenues to develop your network and community—but both are essential for a well-rounded educator. A professional learning network (PLN) comprises those outside your immediate bubble. These people bring in new ideas and speak from different perspectives to find the right solutions for our classrooms. A professional learning community (PLC) acts as the first line of defense. These friends are close-by colleagues who can speak with us about specific issues occurring in our shared space.

Having both a PLC and a PLN is vital if you're planning to live your best educator life! A professional learning community (PLC) is different from a professional learning network (PLN).

A PLN is something you build as a professional using a pedagogical lens. This network challenges your thinking and exposes you to new innovations and perspectives outside of your immediate community. While a PLN does not require proximity, a PLC does.

A PLC is created by people in your immediate surroundings who can help you grow professionally. This group is larger than the big picture ideas but committed to providing specific support. PLCs have norms set by the facilitators. PLCs speak to specifics.

TEACHERS DESERVE A PROFESSIONAL LEARNING NETWORK

RAE SAYS

I have the privilege to have traveled a lot in the last year or so working with schools, and though this may sound a little nuts, I have the same strange moment each and every time my flight takes off. And no, it's not my ears popping in my headphones as I blast my Michael Bublé, Post Malone, John Splithoff, OneRepublic, and John Mayer playlist. (I like a variety of music.)

It's the realization I live in a very small bubble.

When I was offered my dream job early in my career, I knew it was going to change my life. I was going to learn so much. I was going to grow so much. I was going to make such an impact. I was going to change. I was going to be challenged!

Why? Because of the people I was working with.

The dream job building was full of progressive educators killin' it in the field! I was going to soak up everything they'd be willing to teach me!

But what happens when you are not surrounded by teachers all dedicated to their pursuit of better learning for their students? Do you have to accept that stagnant environment stunting your growth?

Absolutely not. In the age of connections and networking, you have the power to choose your colleagues and what you learn from them. Everything you want to know, explore, or see in action is accessible, right now, in a free podcast or YouTube video. Gone are the days when you were forced to change teaching positions to learn the new best practices. Gone are the days when collaboration depended on all the collaborators being near each other. You have the power to bring anything back to your classroom tomorrow, simply through googling.

But you have to know where to look.

RAE SAYS

I remember first connecting with Adam. After my principal handed me the book *Kids Deserve It*, I was hooked. I loved the message, the dream, and the hope it made me feel. Building the right learning atmosphere for teachers was possible, I realized.

So, I did what any young teacher would do . . . I read the book and placed it on my bookshelf after reading.

That was a good read, I thought. *It's too bad it's over.*

During my last semester of my graduate program, I found out I was one course short of graduation. I was not going to let this lapse in judgment hold me back from my intended graduation date. I signed up for the first available class and doubled up my last semester. The course dealt with purposeful technology integration.

The first assignment required me to make an educator social media account. For the sake of a grade and acquiring my master's degree, I begrudgingly created a Twitter account.

Who did I follow first? My favorite educational authors—Dave Burgess and Adam Welcome.

We are sure you've heard it a thousand times before, but a common phrase in personal growth circles is "You are the top five people you surround yourself with."

Who are your top five people? Don't worry, when you ask a teacher, most ask, "Do students count?" and giggle.

The reality is, everyone counts! So, if you had to choose the type of person you wanted to develop into, what type of person would you choose to surround yourself with?

Those who often explore new ideas?

Those who focus on the silver lining?

Those who suck the energy out of the room?

Those who see one side of an argument?

Those who stay open minded?

Those who value diversity?

RAE SAYS

I was not sure what circle was the right circle for me to live within as I began growing my PLN. Nevertheless, I soon learned, the people I thrived around were those who validated my fears, challenged me to take strategic risks, led with a student-focused heart, and identified as "dot collectors."

I first learned about the "dot collector" idea from Jimmy Casas during a *Teach Better Talk* podcast recording. In short, a "dot collector" is someone dedicated to connecting with other people and who aims to connect others. These people focus on supporting everyone they meet in an effort to connect them with others who will lift them up, challenge their thinking, and support their passions.

Who is the best connection you have made? Have you chosen to connect any dots recently to support others' growth and development?

Michael Jennings

Director of Healthy Body and Physical Education Teacher
Idaho

When was the last time you put significant focus, time, and effort into accomplishing something? I mean something that you worked on multiple days in a row, something you cussed at, sweat over, and thought you couldn't do? Something that, at first, was nearly impossible, then with time and effort was borderline doable, then eventually you got it?

And every time after that, you knew you could do it again and again. How did you feel after that? My guess is that the time, energy, and effort was worth every minute and every ounce of sweat! That "hot damn" moment when students realize that with time and effort they can accomplish things that were previously impossible is something special! This is an exciting feeling in any subject! But I'm a physical educator, and I can honestly say when students overcome what they perceive as physical barriers and the impossible becomes probable—that profound moment— that's my "why."

THE FIRST STEP: CHOOSE A PLATFORM

Take the first step toward growing your PLN by creating a profile on social media or a professional networking site. There are a few different ways to do this, but the most important element to focus on is what platform is going to be the best fit for you to consume and create content. For some, this may correlate to your learning preference, while for others audience may be the major driver. Are you looking to connect with students? Ask them what platforms they are most passionate about. Are you looking to connect with like-minded colleagues? Ask them what space they are spending the most time in.

RAE SAYS

I won't lie to you: I have a love-hate relationship with Twitter. It's not that I don't see the value (I have grown *a ton* and made life-changing connections there), but the medium does not serve me well.

Labeled SLD in second grade in reading and writing, I find the fact that Twitter is mostly text-based more challenging. It doesn't mean I don't use it often, but I acknowledge the areas that turn me off from the platform and its connection to an area I am continually striving to better in myself.

Instagram, as an image- and audio-based platform, I find more "Rae friendly." While there are aspects of Instagram I do not enjoy, it's all about finding the right networking platform for you.

Real talk, networking sites will always change. A decade ago, Facebook was the place to be! Now, TikTok is the go-to for our youth. But making connections isn't about the platform you choose. It's about using the tool to form authentic relationships with people who support you and help you get better at what you do. The platform simply serves as the medium to reach your goals.

THE NEXT STEP:
MAKE AUTHENTIC CONNECTIONS

Now that you've slowly stepped out of your comfort zone, it's time to form authentic connections.

So, how do you form authentic relationships? Social media sites can easily turn into echo chambers. Due to News Feed algorithms and drama-focused users, it's easy to be sucked into the hurricane effect of different people sharing the same blanket statements.

Therefore, take purposeful time to connect and intentional time to step away. Your network should be crafted just as intentionally as the top five people you surround yourself with.

Pose questions to your network.

Share celebratory news with your network.

Brainstorm solutions with your network.

And when you find yourself making a strong connection with another person, make sure to follow their account to keep up-to-date on their message.

And once you are continually finding value in what someone in your network is sharing? Pop them a private direct message to share your appreciation! They may take a little while to message you back, but a conversation may emerge, enabling you to dive deeper with shared resources.

RAE SAYS

I actually connected with the Teach Better Team virtually on Twitter. I had no idea a direct message with Jeff Gargas would lead to a life-long friendship.

It's not that I have not made hundreds of connections that had an invaluable impact on my life, but that single direct message led to hundreds of deep educational debates, thousands of connections with other educators, and one introduction to a teaching framework that changed my ability to reach my students better than I had even believed was possible in a public school classroom filled to the brim with students in need of personalized support.

Every moment is an opportunity for a connection.

Go connect!

THE LAST STEP:
STAY CURRENT WITH YOUR PLN

Staying up-to-date with your new network can be tough, given your many commitments over the course of any given week. The reality is, hope is not a strategy. You can't just hope to stay up with anything. Because then, when life gets busy or difficult (like it always seems to), it becomes too easy to allow your hope to fall by the wayside.

Create a plan.

Dedicate thirty minutes each week every Monday or fifteen minutes every day after school to stay current with your network. This could be a minor as watching a quick Instagram Story or participating in a Twitter chat once a month.

Set realistic targets and embed them into your routine.

Why? Because you deserve it.

TEACHERS ALSO DESERVE A PROFESSIONAL
LEARNING COMMUNITY

We all know those moments when you are struggling with a student in your classroom. Being the strong educator you are, you take all the appropriate steps to support this child, who is clearly needing more from you. You fully understand everyone has their own battles we may not know the details of. Therefore, you call home, schedule meetings, and dedicate yourself to building a stronger relationship with them.

And for a while, you feel like you are getting somewhere. For a period of time, something you tried gives you a glimmer of hope. But then the behavior bubbles up again.

What are you missing?

We cannot tackle the world on our own—and our kids deserve educators who can see the value others' insight can provide. Please believe us when we say we're 100 percent pro-teacher, all the way, every day, forever!

We believe that teachers deserve a professional learning community (PLC) made up of people you see on a regular basis in your building, district, or community to brainstorm and problem solve with.

BUILDING YOUR OWN COMMUNITY

Go out and find your people! Whether they are down the hall or a few doors down, it's important for us all to have people we can confide in at a moment's notice! Do not limit your ability to reach your students by being unwilling to allow others to get to know you as a person and share themselves with you.

RAE SAYS

I used to be a master at closing my door and doing what I needed to do in my classroom. For a long time, I thought this was the best (and only) way to really reach my learners. My mindset was that I may not have had control over what was going on outside the walls of my classroom, but within our four walls, we could make anything happen!

So, every moment I had, I closed my door and cut myself off from those down the hall.

Jorge Valenzuela

STEM Educator
Virginia

At Lifelong Learning Defined, my main goal is to effect social change by helping educators become their absolute best for developing students and to equip them with the skills and dispositions needed for successful lives.

I am extremely dedicated to making schools better by helping them align three major areas of focus.

1. Local and federal policies
2. Good teaching practices
3. The needs of the workforce

At the local level, schools and districts are required to implement a host of initiatives into the work they're already doing. And oftentimes they need assistance with how that can occur systemically and logistically in classrooms (either in person or through remote learning). This is where I apply my years of experience as a classroom teacher and district administrator.

In support of good teaching practices in all of the instructional areas, my professional development sessions model for educators how to use evidence-based instructional strategies and vetted educational protocols. These sessions are inspirational, actionable, and fun for participants. Teachers learn to plan and facilitate high-quality instruction through systematic and reflective practices. Some of my session topics include project-based learning, restorative practices, social emotional learning engineering (for STEM), computational thinking and computer science integration, and collaborative lesson planning.

I have found a lot of gratification in my enduring mission at Lifelong Learning Defined and enjoy helping schools grow their capacity to empower and develop our young people into citizens who will be prepared for life in any century!

There is absolutely a time and place to block out the noise, close your door, and take control of the experiences you want to provide students. However, in doing so *all* the time, you run the risk of eliminating a valuable resource for your growth—others' insights!

You do not need to facilitate a classroom the same way as someone else to be able to learn from them. Even the most "outdated" educators have value and insight to provide. It is what we do with this information that can provide the most benefit to our students.

Those types of classroom-altering ideas and collaborations only happen when you get off of Educator Island and build your professional learning network. We realize there is a lot of noise on social media, but if you keep your network professional and education focused, much of the other noise will get filtered out. You're going to get out of it what you put into it, and even twenty minutes a week will provide valuable learning, lifelong connections, and ideas that you just can't find anywhere else.

Here's an example.

ADAM SAYS

I travel a lot and work with hundreds of school districts across the country on a yearly basis, really big districts, and small districts, too.

Recently I was in a very small and very rural district in Missouri. So rural that I didn't have cell phone reception on the drive in. I spent the entire day with all the teachers (about thirty-five) in the district doing an assortment of different professional development sessions and having just an awesome time learning together. Amazing teachers that were doing amazing work with kids, but many of them were not connected.

My schedule was super booked for the day, and we hadn't allocated any time to talk about getting connected with other educators outside of the district. We were talking about makerspaces with the high school teachers (about fifteen in all), and one of them raised their hand to ask some clarifying questions about using drones with students. This teacher had a drone already and just hadn't integrated it into the classroom with kids because they weren't sure where to start.

So I asked the question that I ask every educator when they have a question: "Are you on Twitter?"

A sheepish look came across their face. "I am, but not really," they said. "It's been years since I used my account."

Let me tell you, this is such an ideal circumstance for a presenter. You have someone who at one point in time saw the benefit of Twitter or went to a conference and signed up. But then they stepped away from it, or just never saw the full potential in the first place.

Fast-forward a few minutes while they did the password recovery on their account and this is what I had them do.

"Tweet this from your account: 'High school teacher from MO here, looking for ways to integrate drones into my classroom with students.'"

This particular teacher only had fifteen or so followers, so like I do with everyone, I encouraged them to tag me in their tweet so I could retweet them to my followers in the hopes of getting a larger response from the PLN that I've built over the last ten years.

Within ten minutes, the ideas, links, videos, and more started coming in. After one hour, we had over a dozen responses with curriculum ideas, offers to collaborate, and even a drone company that wasn't too far away.

It is incredibly helpful to have supportive colleagues to talk to on the fly and bounce ideas off of at a moment's notice. These are your go-to people.

The benefit of a PLN is the broad swath of expertise you can bring in, since it is national.

The benefit of the PLC is how close these people are and how quickly you can access them; you can ideally talk to someone in that moment, without having to wait.

Don't choose to allow your PLC to consist only of people who are similar to you. Welcome in all educators from a variety of perspectives to build a well-rounded professional learning community. This will allow you to do more than your best for your students, it will enhance your impact with the support of others along the way.

#TEACHERSDESERVEIT
EDUCATOR EXPERIMENT

Build your PLN by asking questions! Take a moment right now (like right this moment) and post an education question using #TeachersDeserveIt! You could even tag Adam and Rae in the post. Let's use your network to gather resources and get answers!

CHAPTER 9

Teachers Deserve Time, Space, and Technology

As Adam always says, "We cannot teach Wi-Fi kids with landline strategies." We must continue the conversation around teacher wellness and equity, and it's never too late to take it up a notch!

During the COVID-19 pandemic, equity was brought to the forefront of conversations occurring across the nation. On the news, in speeches from public officials, and in conversations among district leadership, a discussion about the discrepancy between student and teacher access to essential tools began to emerge. As teachers managed a shift toward planning for remote learning, we also shifted our mindset toward getting students and families the necessary elements they needed for survival.

Throughout all of this turmoil, teachers persevered. Teachers took action. Teachers made a commitment to serve others—and some did all of these before thinking about serving themselves. The reality, though, missed by many outside of the educational circle, was that this act of commitment did not emerge due to the pandemic. But rather, it was simply brought to light. Educators have been serving others before themselves for decades.

This dedication should be celebrated. And what is the best way to celebrate during a time when educators showed up for families? By granting educators the essentials they need for themselves, mainly time, space, and equitable practices for all students.

Uh-oh, there educators go again asking for support to serve others . . .

TEACHERS DESERVE TIME

Time is like closet space. You use what you have, and you always wish you had more.

ADAM SAYS

Over the last five years, I have had the amazing opportunity to travel the country and work with educators in so many states, in countless school districts and at conferences. There are always similarities no matter where I am, and one theme that comes up all the time was something we also dealt with when I was a classroom teacher and a principal: time.

Time is the currency that teachers want more of.

More time to plan.

More time to assess.

More time to connect with kids.

More time to observe colleagues as a means to learn and grow.

More time to not have a predetermined agenda, and more time to spend with grade levels or department teams as professionals to talk about curriculum, kids, and how to make classrooms more engaging places for students.

More time that should not be spent filling out forms and data protocols that aren't even connected to the work that's happening in the classroom.

ADAM SAYS

Let me tell you something loud and clear. Principals have money in their budgets; I know because I've been one. And just like you do at home with your personal finances, principals decide how and what to spend the money on.

Very quickly into my first year as a principal, I decided we should spend money on time. My office manager and I sat down with the budget, and I told her we needed to find three thousand dollars for substitute teachers.

She responded, "I don't know, Adam, the budget was set last year and money is really tight."

"We need to find three thousand dollars," I said. "Teachers don't have enough collaborative planning time throughout the week where they can simply talk and plan in a creative way, without an agenda from me or someone at central office."

"Okay, okay—we'll find some money somewhere," she said.

And . . . we did!

And it was amazing!

That first year, we gave all grade-level teams one day where we hired substitute teachers and they were allowed to dress in sweats or any kind of comfy clothes they wanted. They all set up basecamp in an empty classroom and planned the entire day. And it was *amazing!*

The directions for their collaboration were simple:

1. Be creative.
2. Talk about kids.
3. Think big.
4. What actions can you take right away, and what are some longer-term initiatives we can discuss in the months ahead?
5. What problems are you currently dealing with that I can help solve?
6. And—enjoy!

I stopped by their planning sessions throughout the day, but it was only to bring them coffee, check in on their conversations, and answer questions—and there were a lot of questions.

Do you know what happens to teachers when you give them paid time, at school, that's not structured or dictated by a laundry list of things they have to do?

Dr. Shamaine Bertrand

College of Education Professor
Illinois State University

When I got to high school, I realized that there was a difference in the experiences that some students had regarding schooling as opposed to others. While this is often the norm, I realized that the common theme was that many students that were labeled marginalized did not receive the same encouragement, resources, and opportunities as their peers. While my initial response was not to be a teacher, after attending college I began to think where I could have the most impact and make a difference.

After a lot of contemplating, I chose to teach. My "why" for this is because I want to make a difference. I want Black and Brown youth who do not always see themselves represented in the classroom to know that they can be anything, that I know what it feels like to feel like the odds are against you and you do not belong, but you can be successful. My nana, Hazel, was the first person that I know of in our family to obtain a bachelor's *and* a master's degree. She was a social worker and still devotes her life to serving her community and helping youth. This was my inspiration for wanting to do well in school and make a difference.

After teaching fourth grade for a few years, I began to think about how I can have a greater impact on education and help to make education equitable for students that are labeled "marginalized" and do not get the effective education they need to be successful. I obtained my PhD, and I became a teacher educator. I am currently an assistant professor of elementary education at Illinois State University. This is my dream job, but it's also the job that allows me to do the work that I believe is needed and that will prepare future teachers to create equitable learning environments that are centered on equity, social justice, and antiracism. The fact that I get to do this at one of the top teacher producers in the United States is why I get out of bed in the morning.

I have had preservice teachers enter my class that have never had an interaction with a Black teacher or have not had any experience working with Black and Brown youth. At the end of the semester, these preservice teachers share with me how their perspectives have changed, and while doing the critical reflective work was hard, they are excited to work on themselves.

My biggest inspiration are the amazing women in my family that support me, encourage me, love me, and believe in me regardless. These women are my mother (Camala), nana (Hazel), aunts (Wendy and Antionette), and paternal grandmother (Hazel). Whether it is a text that says *I love you and you got this* or a card sent in the mail with encouraging words, they motivate me and inspire me to continue doing the work that is needed to make a difference in education.

My first year teaching was at Dumfries Elementary School in Virginia. My class was the most diverse class I ever had. Many of the students in my class were from impoverished backgrounds and had adult responsibilities like raising siblings or taking care of elderly family members. These students were only in fourth grade. I had no idea what I was doing as a teacher in regards to how to get everyone where they needed to be by the end of the year. I decided to be a combination of the teachers that I have had along the way, because I grew up in a low-income community. I built an amazing classroom community where we valued education and worked hard, yet we created a space where we could be our authentic selves and if necessary talk through our issues and problem-solve. Despite what my students were experiencing outside of school, they worked hard, and at the end of the year they showed academic growth. I do what I do to make sure that students like the ones I taught in Dumfries and the ones that grow up like I did get an equitable opportunity in schools.

Teachers are creative.

They come up with amazing and imaginative ideas to implement with their classes.

They connect on a different level because there isn't the pressure of trying to cram everything in during a thirty-minute meeting after school.

They talk about kids and how they can support those students in need and push those that can reach a little higher.

And most of all—teachers are grateful and feel even more respected as professionals. They're grateful that you treated them like professionals by giving them paid time during the school day that was uninterrupted where they could learn and plan and grow together as a team.

ADAM SAYS

After that first year, and every year after that I was at that school, each grade level team got *three* release days to plan and collaborate and work together as a team.

Did those extra days cost more money? Of course they did.

But you can find it somewhere in the budget. You have money; it's all about what you choose to spend it on. We chose to spend a small portion of it on the ability to give teachers professional time with each other. During the school day, without strict parameters, to talk and collaborate with their colleagues.

What if you only have one PE teacher and/or one music teacher?

Connect them with other teachers within or outside of the district. Allow them to take the day off campus to connect and shadow someone at a different school as a way to learn and grow.

RAE SAYS

Anytime I had the opportunity to take a break from my normal day-to-day grind and collaborate with other teachers, I came back the next day fired up with new ideas. During this time our brains were given a chance to operate differently and reconnect with our "why" for entering into education.

Why? Because good teachers enjoy learning, and connecting, and thinking together, and talking about kids like they never have before. Because teachers shouldn't be rushed, and they deserve to be given the freedom as professionals to do so.

We're not getting into the brain research here. But let's think about it on a very simple level for a minute. You've been teaching all day, supporting students, shifting from one subject to the next, and then the bell rings at the end of the day and you're expected to shift your focus from working with students to being around your adult colleagues with a mindset of planning or analyzing data. That's really challenging for most people.

You're being put into the final minutes of a big game, after you just played an entire game at full speed that just ended a few minutes before.

It's unfair to our teachers.

It doesn't make sense.

It's not how you perform or think at your highest level.

And it needs to change.

Dear Leaders,

If you want your teachers to feel like professionals and act like professionals and grow like professionals, we need to treat them like professionals. Give them more time to do just that.

Dear Teachers,

If you are pursuing more for yourself so you can best support your students, advocate like we teach our students to do on a daily basis. Ask for your time. Manage your time. And choose to utilize your time in the most effective way possible.

There are many different ways to treat teachers like professionals. But in my experience, the gift of time is one of the most valuable that you can give them.

ADAM SAYS

I have read too many articles, seen too many videos on YouTube, and been to more companies than I can count, and it's simply just not fair, and something has to change.

Teachers deserve a space to decompress and regroup.

Free food.

Sleep pods.

Laundry services.

A masseuse.

Yoga.

Exercise equipment.

The option to bring their dog to work.

And much more.

Companies are creating office spaces that are not only welcoming to employees, but also help them to relax, decompress, and regroup.

Hungry from the red-eye flight you just took? Grab a snack or something from the salad bar.

Tired from a busy week of meetings? Take a nap in the sleep pod.

Haven't had a chance to do laundry? No worries, we have that taken care of.

Feeling stressed from your new client? Hop into a yoga class or walk on the treadmill to clear your mind.

Now think about a teacher's normal space.

They have thirty kids in their class or 120 across all periods, the lesson they just planned on the Chromebooks bombed because the Wi-Fi was acting up, one of their students is sick and vomited in the garbage can, so now the entire classroom smells, student behaviors have been escalating lately, the materials for the new math program your district is implementing haven't shown up yet, your office manager calls to tell you that three of your kids have lice and they need to check everyone and send a letter home, and the custodian is going to come down right now to vacuum so please take your class to the library.

Where does a teacher go to decompress and regroup?

Nowhere.

Because their principal called saying they're short substitute teachers today and they're not getting a prep and have to cover another class right after lunch. And there aren't any lesson plans, so please bring something for the kids to do for the fifty-minute period.

Real life—teacher life.

More and more recently researchers are publishing articles about how teaching is one of the most stressful jobs someone can have. Then why the heck isn't there a quiet place at schools for teachers to gather their thoughts after an emotional incident in their classrooms, or just because they need to quietly regroup before heading back to their class?

ADAM SAYS

And what about laundry? If I ever become a principal again, I'm going to get washers and dryers installed at my school for teachers to use during the day. How amazing would that be for staff? #GameChanger.

Years ago when I was a principal, a few teachers came to me and wanted to complete a makeover of the staff room at our school. They wanted some money. I didn't have much, but what they did was amazing.

They painted the walls different colors. Cleaned up some old piles that were in the way and made space for some new "relaxed and flexible seating." We talk about flexible seating for students in classrooms—how about in the staff room for teachers, too?

After the makeover, there was a difference in how many teachers spent time in that space. Maybe it was the colorful walls. Or the photos of their families that were now proudly displayed. I'm sure the couches and comfortable seating contributed, too.

If we want teachers to be happy, relaxed, energized, and ready to do the work in the classroom, we need to do a better job of creating spaces for them to relax and recuperate outside of their classroom.

RAE SAYS

Heading back to school in August has always been an exciting time for me.

Am I excited to meet my new students? Yes.

See my colleagues? Yup.

See learning opportunities come to life for students? Of course.

But to be honest, one of the many reasons I defined working as a sixth-grade teacher at Evans Junior High as my "dream job" was because of my administration's dedication to building up the culture of our school. It almost seemed like each year, the team would level up their "great culture game."

In 2019, I walked into an Institute Day eager to see what the year would bring. After a quick welcome focused on our mission to improve the lives of our students, we were grouped into teams by birthday and sent on a scavenger hunt around the building.

"A scavenger hunt?" I questioned. "I have taught in this building for over seven years. I know where everything is."

The truth is, I did know where Room 2165 was and where to find the paper cutter. But it was even more fun to roam around the building to see the new teacher relaxation spaces that had been set up for the year by our leadership team.

There were couches with cute pillows set up with an old-school Nintendo game console in one of the many goofy new spaces we took selfies in that day.

Wow, did I feel appreciated.

Wow, did I feel valued.

Wow, did those spaces come in handy during the tough days of behavior concerns, tough parent updates, and DCFS calls.

Bryan Zwemke

High School Principal
Illinois

What's my "why"? This is a question that drives me to want to get better as an educator. I am inspired by educators and their commitment to students in and out of the classroom. The time, energy, passion, and effort educators put forth to support students is amazing. Education is a very personalized journey, and I am fortunate to be a small part of that journey.

As an administrator, my goal is to support the education ecosystem to allow for growth and change that is meaningful to the educator. Further, my "why" is to support teachers, staff, and students so they may grow and be successful both in the present and in their future on their own.

Education is an exciting and evolving field, which calls for an interdependent approach between teachers, students, staff, administration, and the learning community. My "why" is to be present in the moment and treat each opportunity and encounter with a member of our learning community with respect, compassion, and understanding.

TEACHERS DESERVE SPACE

As educators continue to create spaces to foster progressive student learning, and as businesses continue to find ways to incorporate necessary collaborative spaces, we must also discover ways to build these in for our teachers.

Does building a new collaborative learning pod cost money—yes.

But teachers don't need a fully gutted new interior to build safe spaces for our educators to reset and de-stress.

ADAM SAYS

I have been working with a school district in Long Island for the past two years, and the principal at North High School in Sachem School District has put her money where her words are and created a Zen Room for teachers.

I've seen firsthand what their amazing principal, Patti Trombetta, has created, and she did it all for a few hundred dollars in an old textbook storage room that wasn't being used anymore. Patti has built a space where teachers can relax, recuperate, recharge, and just chill when they need some time. We fully realize that a company with massive budgets has more available money to spend on sleep pods, chefs, and other niceties for employees. And we'll also tell you that you can do what Patti Trombetta has done for a few hundred dollars!

- Tapestries
- Sound machine
- Essential oils
- Music
- Bean bags
- Comfy chairs
- Inspirational quotes
- Rugs

- And other very Zen-like details that just make the space a place you want to go and breathe some new energy into your body.

Think big with your idea for creating a space for teachers to decompress and recharge, but keep it simple if you have limited space and resources, like most schools do.

- Partner with local businesses for furniture
- Encourage afterschool get-togethers at a local yoga studio
- Ask for parent donations
- Search on Craigslist for items; there's always a ton to choose from
- Snag a coffee for a teacher as a surprise to make them smile
- Include mental health support in staff notes
- Write a grant to purchase new items for a staff workroom or classroom
- Offer gym equipment for staff to get physical exercise
- Look at your building in a different way and find a space for teachers
- Check in on staff members having a hard time (not just once, but often)
- Make counselors available to all
- And maybe, as a first step, create an open-door policy to be a support for others

---

TEACHERS DESERVE EQUAL ACCESS TO TECHNOLOGY

In order to prepare students to be twenty-first-century thinkers, problem solvers, collaborators, inventors, and the next generation of creators, teachers cannot use nineteenth-century tools.

Teachers cannot prepare themselves to be relevant thinkers and innovative lesson planners, ready for students, and able to deal with all the constant changes in education with old and outdated equipment and mindsets.

ADAM SAYS

When I was a principal, the school where I took over had *amazing* teachers that were creative, fun, excited about their jobs, and absolutely loved coming to school each and every day.

With that being said, there were some definite gaps when it came to certain curriculum programs that had been implemented with previous administrations, and most glaring was the fact that our district had this huge plan to roll out 1:1 laptops from third grade all the way to twelfth.

I'm not complaining about giving students devices at all, but if we're going to expect teachers to properly implement technology in their classroom in meaningful ways, they have to be the ones to first get the technology access so they're prepared before the kids.

It was 2012. How could anyone back then or now, in 2020, operate without a laptop?

Educators don't "need" to be mobile; they *are* mobile. Constantly on the move throughout the day, teachers need access to tools that will help them be the best educators they can be.

If we want and even expect our teachers to implement pretty much anything in their classrooms, we have to first give them access so they're comfortable and proficient, and then support them in coming up with their own creative ways to develop engaging lessons with their students so they feel comfortable and prepared.

RAE SAYS

I have been fortunate enough to support a number of districts as they work toward a new implementation launch.

Pilot groups are formed, discussions are facilitated, and teachers are provided with training as well as follow-up meetings. These are more than just moments in time when new ideas are provided to teachers. When districts implement a new idea, teachers must feel supported and have time to process through the vision for the implementation.

On the flip side, I have also been a part of a few districts who chose to take an opposite approach—taking an idea, moving quickly, and implementing it from the top down.

- This year we are going 1:1 (little training/discussion provided)
- This year we will be going to standards-based grading (little training/discussion provided)
- This year we are going to be using a new LMS platform (little training/discussion provided)

Would you teach a student in this disjointed way?

Scenario: A district is spending hundreds of thousands of dollars on laptops for students, and the teachers have outdated desktops in their classrooms.

Probable outcome: Not successful.

If you want something to be successful, you must properly prepare and equip people with the tools to give them a chance at success.

ADAM SAYS

Back in 2012, I shifted a bunch of money around in my budget, asked my parent group for some financial help, and bought every single teacher at our school a MacBook Air. There wasn't enough money to buy them all at once, and since the initial laptop rollout for students was in the upper grades, that's where we started. Then six months later we bought laptops for all the primary teachers, and it made such a profound difference across the board.

Teachers had the access they needed. They brought their laptops to grade-level meetings, staff gatherings, a table in the back of the room when working with students one-on-one, and of course home. They brought them to professional development training and conferences on the weekend so they didn't need to take notes with a yellow legal pad—c'mon, it was 2012!

There were definite grumblings at the central office about this one, but I didn't care. We trust our teachers with 20 or 30 or 180 kids every single day; we should have that same level of trust with equipment that will make them more proficient teachers. With this approach, teachers feel respected.

Without teachers having a laptop of their own, the students would have more access than the teachers did. How does that make any sense at all? Teachers will be far more inclined to implement technology in their classrooms with students when they have access to the tools and can explore them.

We talk all the time in education about equity, and rightfully so the conversation is often all about the kids. We're going to tell you, though, that teacher equity is so very important as well. Teacher equity is important, and so is teacher access. Access to the supplies we need without having to beg, borrow, steal or write endless grants for classroom basics.

Teachers need access to proper Wi-Fi so they can implement the programs and online content that's expected of them. Access to furniture that gives their students more seating options that in turn will help to make them more successful students. And access to the support they and their students need on a daily basis—counseling, intervention, snacks, breakfast, lunch, emotional support, and everything else that is needed to support our children.

Teachers can't mold the next generation of thinkers if they don't have equitable access to what will help them be successful.

NEXT STEPS

We are well aware that schools and districts don't have all the funding they need to properly equip teachers. But our belief about effective implementation models to support teachers to better support their students still stands.

RAE SAYS

One of my favorite things to work on with districts is finding the most effective way to implement a new idea districtwide. No matter the initiative, no matter the district size, no matter the culture, a new successful initiative implementation must begin with a few key elements in order to be successful.

- A clear vision for the implementation
- Teacher buy-in—often earned through multiple pilot groups
- Time for facilitated discussion
- Training for teachers and stakeholders

The reality is, teachers are put on the front lines to communicate and educate their students and stakeholders. The more we can take this responsibility off of them to allow them to actually facilitate instruction in the classroom, the more successful we will be.

It takes a united front.

#TEACHERSDESERVEIT EDUCATOR EXPERIMENT

1. It's a common practice to ask students to sketch out their ideal learning environment, so let's twist this for an activity for you! Build your ideal relaxation space! Start with a blank piece of paper and four walls. Sketch out what an ideal relaxation space would look like.

   Then, just as you think you are done, think bigger! Include every dream possible in this sketch. Wishing for a waterfall? Throw it in there! Wishing for ten fluffy puppies? Sketch that in! Dream big audacious dreams! Share your sketch out using #TeachersDeserveIt as you reflect on why you included each one of the elements you chose. What does this space feel like? How can you take small elements of your image and slowly craft it into a reality? Do not limit your creativity. You deserve it.

CHAPTER 10
Teachers Deserve Boundaries

You've heard it before, but we'll say it louder for the people in the back: we need healthy boundaries between work and home!

We understand this is easier said than done, and we do not expect for your balance to look 50/50. But boundaries are essential. The stress of teaching can be overwhelming, so you cannot continue to bring it home to your families. You have the right to say no when needed and find your happy space. No more teacher guilt.

TEACHERS DESERVE TO LEAVE IT IN THE CLASSROOM

Imagine that the bell rings and your students hustle out the school doors. You spend the appropriate amount of time waving goodbye, making small talk with your colleagues, and getting a quick update on a student from your administrator.

Walking back to your desk, you notice your to-do list and full email inbox. You spend fifteen minutes taking care of a few items, writing that necessary update on a student's success and printing that thing you need for the following day.

As you glance down at your watch, you have a choice to make: beat your family home and spend the night with them making dinner and being a part of the story before bed, or text your spouse or book club friends that you will be late because you have other things to accomplish here at work.

See, we've all been there . . .

When that student had a meltdown.

When that item was brought up about next year, which drastically affected your placement.

When that colleague shared their unwelcome opinion.

When you had to make that call to the police.

When that lesson went the wrong way.

When you had that parent phone call that turned sour.

When that to-do list item had not been crossed off.

When that copy run didn't happen.

What do you choose?

ADAM SAYS

In my first book, *Kids Deserve It*, we wrote a chapter called "Leave It in Your Car," the premise of which was that every teacher has something going on in their life that could potentially be brought into their classroom and cause some type of negativity. Bring your best self to school every single day so you'll be the best for your students. That chapter was true when we wrote it and still is today.

Here's something else to consider: all teachers should leave it in their classrooms.

Your classroom is important. Your students are important. Your district and community are important. But without you, none of it means anything. You, your family, your friends, your activities, and your home life—they're more important.

When you're done teaching for the day—leave what happened at school in your classroom.

Leave the stress of standardized testing; there's only so much you can do about it anyway.

Leave the heartache and anguish you may feel for the home lives that some of your students have to deal with, and return tomorrow to care about them like you always do when they're in your class.

Leave the emails that you haven't yet answered; they'll still be there tomorrow.

Leave the argument you may have had with a colleague or administrator; you deserve to go home and clear your head and can deal with it tomorrow.

Leave that unsettling feeling you have about the new district-adopted curriculum, and use it as a guide to teach your students while you bring in differentiated learning opportunities so all kids can access the curriculum.

Leave it all. Prep the materials you'll need for tomorrow. Lock your classroom door. Put a smile on your face, and hold your head up high. And go enjoy the rest of your day.

You deserve it!

Teaching is an extremely demanding, fun, and at times stressful job, and if we can't separate our professional from our personal lives and nurture them both in different ways in order to be happy and balanced human beings, then something needs to change.

You, your family, your friends, and your neighbors deserve someone who can laugh and connect and leave their work in the classroom. And the magic question is "How do I leave it all in my classroom?"

You just do.

You tell yourself that today with your students was awesome, and now your own family needs you.

You look back on the day and find three things to celebrate, and you'll go back tomorrow and do it again.

You take three Post-it notes and leave nice messages on a student's desk so they'll feel positive and ready to go in the morning.

You grab your to-do list and highlight the first two things you are going to focus on when you arrive back in your classroom the following morning so you know exactly where to begin.

You put your papers in a nice stack to the right and left so you can walk into a stress-free environment tomorrow.

You write a nice message to your custodian on the white board to give them an extra smile.

You create a short fifteen-second video telling your students how much fun you had today learning with them and post it to wherever you share information with your class.

You do all this because you have to.

You do all of this so you can leave it in your classroom.

RAE SAYS

In every other chapter of this book, Adam and I have focused on the work we as teachers have to do in making the "Deserve It" statement a reality. The truth is, teachers may deserve it, but we are the only ones that are going to make this a reality. I am so sick of relying on other people to make my dreams come true. I am just about going out and doing it myself!

But this chapter is different. We won't offer you strategies here. The only thing we want you to hear loud and clear in this chapter is this: quit feeling teacher guilt.

You are hardworking. You are making an impact. And regardless of all the good, many of us experience guilt when we close our classroom door and choose family to fill our evenings. When we cannot make all of our hopes and dreams happen and clear our to-do lists from a day's work, guilt creeps in as we get into our cars in the parking lot.

Sometimes we cannot do it all—and that's okay! You're human. Feeling guilty about choosing to focus on those outside your classroom after hours is not serving you in any way.

Look at it this way: right now, you are modeling for your students that they are the most important people in your life, that you are dedicated to creating the most outstanding learning experiences for them that exist in the world.

But you are also modeling for them that if you cannot reach the target you set for yourself that day, you should feel ashamed. You are teaching them this thought process: "Go out and make a great impact in others' lives, but if you do not do it all, each and every day, feel bad."

Stop communicating an unhealthy pattern between work and home life to your students.

Friends, teacher guilt does not belong in your evening routine.

You can and will still be an amazing teacher for the students in your class when you return.

We want you to be an amazing human being for the people in your personal life, too.

TEACHERS DESERVE TO SAY NO

We're just going to keep it real—teachers also deserve to pace themselves.

Because a school year is *not* a sprint. It is a really long marathon with a whole bunch of other activities thrown in there just for fun while you're wearing teacher clothes and trying to do a hundred other things.

Marathon, not a sprint. You gotta set a sustainable pace.

You can't do it all the first couple months of school—you have to pace yourself.

You can't try every single new program or app or website you find—you have to pace yourself.

You can't try to be everything to everybody—you have to pace yourself.

You can't really believe that you're going to get it all done and perfectly right away, or during your first couple of years—you have to pace yourself.

Donna Bussell

Reading Specialist
Oklahoma

My grandfather would tell me stories of when he was in school. He would get his knuckles struck with a ruler or worse for speaking his Native Apache language. His eyes would grow heavy as he remembered these harsh times. But then he would smile and say, "But there was one teacher who was good to me. She was an English teacher with red hair. She knew I wasn't good in English, but she always made me feel smart. She was good to me and was the only one who believed in me." A smile would come across his face, and he would look at me: "You should become a teacher." So, I did, and I try to make every student believe in themselves like that teacher did for my grandfather.

RAE SAYS

In my first few years in the profession, I was a twenty-four-hour teacher. At the time, I was living alone with my cat, Joe, in a small town I had never heard of until I was offered my first job. So, in a new environment and with a new teaching position, I committed full force.

I would arrive at school at 6:00 a.m. and leave around 7:00 p.m. each day. Then, I'd go home to check on my cat and head out again to see my students' basketball games, grab dinner with students' families, join multiple meetings with kids at the Boys and Girls Club, or head back to my classroom to set up for another crazy activity the following day.

I would essentially only head home to sleep and see Old Man Joe.

I was trying to do everything.

I was trying to be everything.

I was trying to be involved in everything.

I was trying to do it all.

And, whether I would admit it or not, I was on a crash course toward burnout.

Teachers are naturally passionate.

Teachers are naturally generous.

Teachers want to be helpful.

Teachers want to be involved.

Teachers want to do what is best for students.

It seems to be a recurring trend.

ADAM SAYS

I am a pusher. My wife calls me a gunner because I'm constantly looking ahead and outward to remain relevant and be first to market with new ideas if I feel they're good for kids and teachers.

Even though I'm self-diagnosed as having too much energy, I had to develop the discipline to pace myself.

During my years as a principal, my staff got very used to new ideas and trying out new programs across our school with tons of excitement. We got to the point where they were the ones bringing in new ideas, which as a leader is exactly where I wanted to be.

It's easier than ever to find new fun and exciting ideas to try out in your classroom, and that's where the problems can sometimes arise. We turn into squirrels, chasing shiny new projects, and then we're trying to implement 10–15 things mediocrely, when we should be focusing on 3–5 and implementing them intentionally and well.

I can remember one such conversation years ago with a teacher named Renee, who would often talk shop with me about our school and its vision for the future.

"Adam," she would say, "we should do this with that grade level because they really need it!"

"Not now," I would reply.

"Adam, there's a new software system that can help us to track reading scores and then provide better intervention for our students."

"Not now," I would reply.

I could tell Renee was somewhat frustrated with my lackluster response, and she probably questioned my sanity because she was so used to me pushing, pushing, pushing on a daily basis.

Have the discipline to see the entire picture. Know that if you bring on those new programs that your school inevitably needs, it's going to add additional strain on teachers, support staff, and even your students if it's too premature. And pace yourself!

Jennifer Rhoades

Fourth-Grade Teacher
Missouri

Like many teachers, it's hard to say there is one reason I decided to become a teacher. I wanted the privilege of impacting kids' lives every day. I wanted to help students realize their voice, find their strengths, and develop big dreams for their life. Teachers encourage, grow, and inspire students to see that they are capable of amazing things. As a teacher now, my goal every day is to reach at least one student in a positive way. There are so many things that can overshadow the reasons why I started teaching. Whether it be meetings, testing, lesson plans, conferences, challenging students, grading—the list goes on. It's easy to let hard things take over. That is why it is important that I never forget my "why" or my purpose.

During my third year of teaching, the reason I teach became even more clear. My dad unexpectedly passed away during the school year. There were days it was hard, and I wondered, *Am I even making an impact?* I was unable to see the good that would come from this hardship. My "why" became blurred by the grief I was walking through.

Many students have now walked through my classroom door who are facing similar trauma in their lives. I am able to empathize with my students through their pain and show them that they are going to be okay. I am able to relate with these kids in a special way, a way my colleagues might not be able to. I have learned that all students need to feel that they are seen and belong so they can learn to their fullest potential and become who they were created to be. I teach so I can show students that their circumstances do not define them, but instead they define how they are going to use their circumstances.

THE MASON JAR

Here's an idea to help you decide how to allocate your team's energy: Give every single teacher at your school a Mason jar, three large rocks that will fit into the jar, three to five medium rocks that will fit into the jar, and then a couple handfuls of sand.

The three large rocks are the big ideas or initiatives that you, the teacher, want to implement in your classroom. We're using a Mason jar because you can't fit more than three big rocks into the jar, or it will break. We must pace ourselves with how many big and special rocks are put into the jar, because a broken jar is the same as a stressed-out and frustrated teacher that doesn't want to come to work.

The medium rocks are those projects or initiatives that maybe you've been doing for a few years, and you feel really confident about where you are with the amount of time they take to plan and implement in your classroom. Don't put more than three or five of those medium rocks in the jar, or it will break. You have to pace yourself with how many medium rocks you bring into your special jar, because a broken jar is the same as a teacher who is snapping at kids and just feeling down in the dumps.

The sand represents everything else that kind of just happens around you. It's the small routines that maybe we take for granted. Or the lessons that don't need much instruction and get very few questions. Please be careful not to put too much sand in your jar. Because if you do, you're going to suffocate and not be able to breathe. You'll feel lost and have no compass to guide you. You'll be at mile 22 of that marathon with no food or water, and you'll have no idea how you're ever going to run those last 4.2 miles.

Please don't put yourself in that situation.

Please tell your colleagues to slow down.

Please tell your principal that right now isn't the time.

Please tell your parent community that another event at night is too much and will really hurt your family time.

Please pace yourself.

Please ask for help when it's needed.

Please slow down if you have to.

Please take time for yourself.

Please be okay with giving 85 percent if you really can't give 100 percent.

RAE SAYS

I talk with my students all the time about how it's not possible for anyone to give 100 percent all the time. So, I do not ask students to give 100 percent each day. Rather, I ask them to give Today's Best.

Today's Best is the best a person can give throughout their day. Sometimes Today's Best is only 90 percent of their typical effort, because they are struggling with things outside of class. Sometimes Today's Best is asking the student to operate at 60 percent or even 70 percent.

Rather than set an unrealistic expectation when the going gets tough, simply offer the best you can for that day, at that moment. That is all you can do.

Then, you start fresh the following day.

To be transparent, 2019 was the most challenging year of my life. I felt as though I was on a rollercoaster each and every moment of the day someone else was controlling. Professionally, I had so many incredible moments of celebration, and personally, I struggled more than I ever had emotionally. Counseling sessions filled my calendar, and I found myself choosing to distance myself from many people I cared for.

But if you look at the year's worth of content I put out to support teachers, if you look at the keynote speeches and professional development sessions I facilitated, if you look at the live videos I ran each week to host Q&A sessions with educators, you didn't see much of a struggle.

Why? It wasn't because I am fake. It wasn't because I was being inauthentic.

It was because I took the advice I continue to give my students each day and gave Today's Best.

Think about the long game, and be in it for the long haul.

Fill your calendar with things that fuel you, and ask for support when you find yourself feeling overwhelmed.

Set long-term goals and pace yourself as you work through them.

Teachers deserve it.

#TEACHERSDESERVEIT EDUCATOR EXPERIMENT

Today is the day!

1. For the next fifteen minutes, write down the top five things that generate teacher guilt for you. Make a list. Then over the next few weeks, work toward letting go of one of your items each week.

   No one said it would be easy—and there may be a few items that are easier to take on then others, but that's okay! Start small and work your way up! Then, share with us how that feels and join in the community of educators giving themselves the benefit of the doubt using #TeachersDeservelt.

CHAPTER 11

Teachers Deserve Fun and Comfort

We all know what stress feels like, but we cannot do our jobs well if we're stressed out all the time. That inevitably leads to burnout and makes the important job we have to do all the more difficult. So let's put a little more fun in our days to make sure we survive the heart work teachers dedicate themselves to. Teachers deserve fun!

FUN WITH YOUR LESSONS

"Oh, I am so excited. I'd love another worksheet!" said no student ever. Learning is meant to be interactive and messy. Add more fun to your next lesson by exploring a new learning opportunity structure.

What makes a lesson fun? There are so many ways to differentiate and engage your students, and how you approach all of that is key. Look at what other teachers in your building are doing, and incorporate elements of what they do into your lessons. Social media can be an amazing laboratory of different ideas, so learn from others and be sure to share what you're doing as well. And if nothing else, just look at your classroom from different angles all the time. We can tend to become creatures of habit, and that's when monotony can take hold and creativity and new ideas go out the door, and we want those to stay inside our classroom!

Try something small like using a new tool to enhance students' experience! Rather than providing students a piece of paper with problems on it, cut up the problems and hide them around the room for students to find. Kick off your next lesson with a funny meme. Record your own TikTok video to try something outside your comfort zone! Connect with a classroom from across the world and explore how their students learn the same topics you and your students are studying. Invite a community member into your classroom to bring relevancy to your lesson. Add a mystery hook days before the lesson for students to wonder about! Jump up on a desk today or skip around the room! Put your lesson in a song and sing it loud and proud like a rock star!

Want to take it up a notch? Incorporate your students' five senses into your next lesson plan! What can they taste, smell, touch, see, and hear to add a new degree of fun to the equation?

Whichever you choose, make learning fun (not only for the students, but for yourself, too)!

FUN WITH YOUR PROFESSIONAL LEARNING

Learning shouldn't be painstakingly boring, and neither should teachers' professional learning.

We want to be inspired!

We want tactical takeaways!

We want relevant topics!

We want a party!

And guess what? All of that can be fun!

Start facilitating teacher learning the same way you do student learning.

Staff meetings and professional learning can be boring—that's the reality for a lot of people. Spice it up and do something different for those times when you get together with your colleagues. Everyone will thank you and appreciate the change of pace!

Add a hook to your next professional learning session. Try out a new tech tool to add a new experience to the opportunity. Integrate media to convey your message. Get people up and moving! Use a GIF to share the emotions you want teachers to feel. Utilize social media. Have someone Skype into the session from another state.

Get the learning juices going!

FUN WITH YOUR NETWORKING

Teachers, connecting with others is supposed to be enjoyable! So let's take networking up a notch!

At your next networking event, be the introduction king/queen. Make it your mission to introduce everyone in attendance. Whether this be a social gathering with your school building or a networking event at a conference after the sessions are finalized, help people mingle by adding a fun and personal touch to the affair.

People enjoy feeling included.

People enjoy talking about themselves.

People enjoy compliments.

People enjoy feeling like they are a part of something larger than themselves.

Be the dot connector.

Want to add fun to your networking virtually? It's time to join an interactive conversation! Consider hopping on a Twitter chat with your favorite follows. Challenge yourself to greet everyone in the chat and learn more about them as human beings. Add a GIF to each of your responses to add a bit of humor to your thoughts. And include celebrations as well as questions within your conversation.

Needing a little more fun? Blast some music in the background and jam out while you collaborate with friends virtually. Music can help keep your mind active!

Rebecca Thal

Fifth-Grade Teacher
New Jersey

I was busy working in corporate America in the early aughts and was caught up in the rat race. I was stuck in this cycle of working very long hours, commuting back and forth to NYC, and managing demanding clients. It was giving me complete anxiety, and at the end of the day I had to ask myself, "For what?" The work I was doing was gratifying in some senses, but it was not changing lives. It was not making a difference given the amount of time and effort I was putting in. That's when I considered other career options where I felt I might actually be able to make a difference. I had a few family members who worked in education, and I was teaching CCD at my church. Many people told me, "You'd make a great teacher," but I never really understood why. After much consideration and research, mainly on my train rides, I decided to quite literally quit my day job and go back to school full time. I received my Master of Arts in Teaching degree in 2005 and never looked back.

While my job now is far from stress free, it is unquestionably more gratifying knowing that the work I do impacts young lives every day. My first few classes of students are now adults. I remember how green I was, looking back on that time, but what I've come to realize is that those young students didn't see that at all. When they run into me around town and give me a big hello, all they remember is how much they liked school. They even quote funny little sayings I have! They remember that I cared . . . and not just about their grades. When I think back to some of my favorite teachers growing up, I distinctly remember how much they cared, too. I also remember their passion, dedication, and commitment to the profession. So I guess when people used to tell me I'd make a great teacher, that's what they meant. This job is about so much more than just delivering content.

FUN WITH YOUR COLLEAGUES

We like to think of fun with colleagues kind of like speed dating. Bear with us for a minute. Teaching usually isn't all that collaborative. Most of the time it's teachers, alone in their rooms with students; they're not talking or connecting with their colleagues. So make some time each time you're together to speed date for a minute with a few different colleagues so you become connected in a new and fun way.

Y'all need to make sure to share the fun with your colleagues as much as possible! These are your people! The ones in the trenches with you—day in, day out. So, let's add in a bit of pizzazz!

Set up a Fall Friend event and give one another small surprise gifts for a full week! Then guess who had whom.

Organize a colleague happy hour! No work talk here. Simply relax and talk about hobbies and family. Allow everyone the opportunity to get to know one another on a personal level!

Organize a surprise donut morning for teachers. Who doesn't love a little sugary pick-me-up on a rainy Thursday?!

Have a step challenge with your colleagues throughout the month. Whoever gets the most steps wins the Golden Shoes for the month to display in their classroom. This also encourages activity and healthy choices with your students.

Create a funny tradition and allow it to be a team inside joke all year long! One of Rae's favorites was administration hiding their school photos around the building. All of the sudden you'd catch one under a poster, on a ceiling tile, or inside a book and get a good giggle.

Do birthdays and anniversaries the right way with a sweet treat or lunch out of the building!

Regardless of what you choose, try and find a way to have some form of fun with your colleagues once a week.

FUN WITH YOUR LEADERSHIP TEAMS

As Rita Pierson said, "People don't learn from people they do not like." This just as true for students as it is adults! So, let's have some fun with our leadership teams! Regardless of the hierarchy in the district, we are all humans, and we all need to see each other as the fun-loving human begins we are!

Consider trading roles for a day. Usually a leadership team consists of the building principal and teacher leaders from different departments and grade levels. So if you want to have fun and learn about what others are going through, switch places for the day or a few hours, and then debrief about what it's like. You'll have fun and gain huge perspective from your colleagues.

Go build a relationship with everyone who's a part of the ecosystem of your building, and find ways to have fun!

Craft an inside joke between you and your administrator.

Invite your leadership team to partake in activities where you are having fun with your colleagues.

Have a coach take part in a student team day activity.

Invite the superintendent to crawl on the floor with students as they play Hungry Hungry Hippos with multicolored balls, scooters, and laundry baskets.

You will be a stronger team when you can share in the fun together.

FUN WITH YOUR OUTFITS

Today is the day—go get out your ugly sweater, lab coat, or pink boa! Add some fun to your lesson this week by dressing the part with a little extra sparkle.

Whether you hunt down new purple glitter glasses, a bright yellow raincoat, or footie pajamas, allow your outfit to add a new element of fun to your plans this week.

Sure, you should make it an intentional incorporation (no one needs you to wear your PJs to work on a Tuesday just because you didn't feel like getting dressed), but allow your outfit to match students' learning!

Are you exploring maps of the United States? Put on your best explorer outfit and Indiana Jones hat!

Are you evaluating number sense? Put on your doctor gear and dissect each number's value!

Are you reading a spooky book? Roll out the witch costume and find some green face paint!

Are you cooking with fractions? Everyone loves a good baker's hat and warm cookies!

How about wearing cowboy boots, Converse, or flip-flops one day? That sounds like fun, and anyone can put their own variation on it.

Allow your outfit to add a new element of fun! Break up the routine, make things less dull, have multiple dress-up days in a given week. Clothes are an expression of how people are feeling and their personalities, so don't just give students permission—invite them to try something different and fun.

FUN WITH YOUR STUDENTS

We all understand content is important, but don't allow your responsibility to teach standards to hinder the fun in your classroom with your students!

Your class will look at you differently when they see you in a different light, so have fun. Be silly, change your voice, dress up, don't talk for an entire day, and just use hand signals. The school year is 180 days long. Having fun and breaking up the routine will add some spice and give you a chance to build stronger relationships with your students.

Introduce a goofy ice-breaker to kick off a Monday morning!

Turn a lesson into a game.

Play music before school and dance with the kids as they start the day.

Explore a new idea with students who have not yet mastered it and work together to figure it out!

Create an inside joke with a student you can refer to at a moment's notice!

Take a line out of CJ Reynolds's book and go snag a package of googly eyes! As students walk up and down the hall, stick a googly eye on them and sarcastically utter, "I've got my eye on you."

It doesn't always have to be innovative.

It doesn't always have to be a grand show.

It doesn't always have to take time to prep.

Just make it real, be yourself, and make sure to end on full-belly giggle!

TEACHERS DESERVE TO WEAR JEANS

This section may seem trivial to some people, but we think it's a really important conversation that needs to be had. And this mindset has the ability to permeate other areas of your organization if you're open minded enough to allow it!

We're just going to say it: teachers deserve to wear jeans to school.

ADAM SAYS

I have traveled a lot around the United States and have had the opportunity to visit hundreds of different schools and districts over the years while doing some really meaningful and fun work with teachers.

With all those visits, you can imagine the differences each organization has. From past practices that have been accepted and part of the culture for years, to other norms that may seem completely out of the ordinary, to how you may do things where you live.

One conversation that continues to baffle me wherever I visit is the conversation and stance on educators wearing jeans to work. It's time to change the conversation and perception of jeans.

People get almost as worked up about this as they do when they tackle the age-old cursive conversation. Either you're completely for cursive, or completely against—there doesn't tend to be too much middle ground in how people feel.

The cursive conversation may very well be an important one, but jeans are as well.

Teachers, principals, directors, and even superintendents should be allowed and possibly even encouraged to wear jeans.

In California as a teacher, my colleagues and I would wear jeans to work at least three days a week. I would wear a nice polo shirt or pocket T-shirt on top and some comfortable shoes.

Teachers don't work in an office. They don't sit in a cubicle all day long.

They're on the carpet interacting and teaching kids.

Teachers are doing bus duty in the rain, snow, and 100-degree weather.

They're doing recess duty on the playground, and there's a pretty high probability they may just get a little dirty from time to time.

Jeans are professional and often expensive. They can cost hundreds of dollars. Jeans are comfortable, and they can be accessorized with a nice button-up shirt or sweater. Jeans are now worn by CEOs that run Fortune 500 companies.

They don't need to be dry-cleaned. Jeans don't tell the whole story, and they don't define you. They don't make someone an ineffective teacher.

We're willing to bet that kids don't care if you wear jeans to work.

ADAM SAYS

I have been on phone calls with superintendents and their executive cabinet and have had others in the room that know me send a text message before the call asking me not to talk about jeans.

"The superintendent doesn't like jeans; please don't bring them up."

What does that even mean? I'm an educator, author, speaker, and consultant. Why the heck would I talk about jeans?

That's when it really started to make sense that there was a bigger issue that needed to be addressed.

Adam spoke in a large school district years ago as their kickoff at the beginning of the school year. The place was packed with amazing educators that were passionate about teaching the next generation of kids. The energy was palpable!

Prior to him speaking there were some speeches from cabinet members, and even someone on the school board got up to make a few announcements. The school board member started by telling the thousand-plus teachers in the room that the school board had just approved a 5 percent raise that was going to be retroactive to last school year and everyone would be getting that check in the coming months and their next paycheck would reflect the raise.

On a scale of 1–10, with one being weak, five being mediocre, and ten being the most excitement you've ever felt in your life, the reaction from the teachers was maybe a five.

What happened next blew him away. The board member then announced that the district administration was going to allow teachers to wear jeans for the next month as school leadership continued a conversation about whether jeans were okay in the long run.

The auditorium *erupted* in the loudest ten celebration that you've ever heard in your life. If you had tried talking to the person sitting next to you, they wouldn't have been able to hear you—it was that loud!

The 5 percent raise garnered a five on the excitement scale, but the fact that teachers in this district could now wear jeans to work? *That* was a ten. It was one of those moments where you realized what was really important to people.

Getting a raise is super important, and it was to them. But this district made a second game-changing decision that day to improve school culture that didn't cost them a dime.

Imagine if that superintendent had immediately jumped on that moment, taken the microphone, and made an executive decision to seize some major social capital. The school board member was in favor, the thousands of teachers were obviously in favor, so what else is there to talk about?

He might have said, "I can see from the reaction of our amazing teachers that this is really important to you. I've just made an executive decision, and from now on during my tenure as superintendent, you can wear jeans to work."

Can you say HERO!?

Maybe you're not as quick to make a decision as we would be, but at least start or revisit the conversation. Don't form a committee or task force. Have conversations with people, and get to the root of why whatever is being done is being done that way.

Don't overthink it.

Humanize it.

Be analytical.

Create a small test group of teachers who are allowed to wear jeans for a week and then ask the students if they felt their teacher was different, or they respected them less.

We are willing to bet they won't even notice—because it's not important to them, which means it shouldn't be important to us.

RAE SAYS

At school one day, as I was working on this chapter during my lunch break, I became curious. Did students actually notice my choice of pants? Did they have an opinion about it?

"Hey guys, do you remember that book I am working on?" I asked my fifth hour.

"Yes of course, Mrs. Hughart! It's your 2020 goal!" a student announced.

"All right, I have to know, how do you feel about teachers wearing jeans? Does it affect your respect for them?"

They looked at me with confused faces. Some of the students giggled in the back of the room. This led to a funny discussion between me and my sixth graders.

The conclusion? They thought the question was so silly. They didn't care at all and saw no difference between black work pants and nice jeans.

The conversation moved from there into a discussion about what kind of outfit would be unprofessional or seem disrespectful. It was so interesting to hear their thoughts.

My favorite comment? "Jeans are awesome, Mrs. Hughart. But don't come to school in a crop top or leggings. That would be so unprofessional!"

Noted. (Duh!)

In society, respect is manifested in different ways depending on your culture.

Years ago, jeans were not viewed as a professional dress option in the same way that women were frowned upon for wearing pants. The item of clothing itself was not the problem. Jeans themselves are not "unprofessional," but there are a number of social and cultural associations attached to denim.

The truth is, this is the case for a number of societal norms.

Wendy Hankins

Reading Interventionist
Texas

Kids are my "why" . . . and I want to be theirs. I want to be that teacher kids run off the bus to say hi to in morning. I want to be that teacher who teaches kids beyond the curriculum. I want to be that teacher who transforms lessons into long-lasting experiences and makes learning fun. I want to be that teacher who lifts kids up, empowers kids, inspires and drives them. I want to be that teacher kids trust. I want to be that teacher kids know believes in them. I want to be that teacher kids come back to visit when they have graduated from high school. I want to be that teacher who inspires a kid to grow up and be a teacher. I want to be that teacher kids remember for good reasons. I want to be that teacher who changes lives. I want to be that teacher you wish you would have had as a kid. I want to be that teacher you want for your own kids. I want to be that teacher that inspires kids to believe in themselves. I want to be that teacher who is unforgettable . . . and for all the right reasons. I want to be that teacher who changes at least one kid's world forever.

RAE SAYS

Each year, I design units that blend my content in with real-world internships. Why? Well, for one thing, I do it because it allows me an avenue to teach students essential skills. Essential skills, in 2020, are viewed in our society as an avenue to respect and responsibility. Students in my classroom practice skills like offering a strong handshake, making eye contact, and using good volume when speaking.

Are these skills important for people to understand? Of course! But why?

Well, because there are many ways in our culture to show respect and responsibility, and I want my students to understand how to play the game of life so they won't be held back by the way their version of respect manifests.

So my question is, will this still be the case a decade from now? Or will there be a new way for people to show respect and be appropriate?

CONCLUSION

Dear Teachers

Dear Teachers,

We wrote this book for you. We want you to feel seen. We want you to feel empowered. And, more than anything else, we want you to hear the cheering happening behind you as we act as your coaches to encourage you to pursue more and go after what you deserve.

We also wrote this book for your students, for your principal, for the families in your community, and even for your superintendent so they have a better understanding of what you're going through and how we think.

This is the start of a conversation around some topics we all know are important, but for some reason they aren't at the forefront of what we're actually talking about in education. That needs to change.

We wrote this book so hopefully you stop feeling "teacher guilt" and remember how important you are as a human being and a teacher. Your students and your school are so very important, but your well-being as a human is more important, and we don't want you to forget that.

We wrote this book because teachers have the most important job in the world. Teaching is more important than being a politician, the CEO of some large company, and it's maybe even more important than being a parent. Because if you add up all the time children spend at school, it's often more than some kids spend at home with their parents—that's pretty important, and so are teachers.

We wrote this book because videos are powerful, blog posts have impact, and messages posted on social media can change lives—but there's nothing like a book that you and your colleagues can read and have a discussion about that will hopefully lead to lasting change for our educational system.

We wrote this book because for far too long education has been put on the back burner. There are many accomplishments to celebrate, but there are so many needs that we've identified that for some reason haven't improved. Schools don't have adequate funding to support all kids, and teachers don't nearly make enough money to survive or thrive financially. There are too many programs voted on and implemented by people who haven't set foot in a classroom since they were students themselves. The list goes on and on. We as teachers are solution-minded people, so we must use that mindset to now find solutions for what ails our educational system. Because we deserve that.

We wrote this book because our voices matter in terms of amplifying our message, but we also wanted to amplify the message of educators all over the country. Teachers are human beings that have families, they have needs and wants, they have different reasons for working in education, but most of all—they're people. They're people that want to make a difference in the life of a child, and that "why" behind what they do must be told so people see who they are and the conversation changes.

We wrote this book because our perspective is unique. Rae is a middle school math teacher and also part of the Teach Better Team, and she travels the country giving professional development workshops to teachers. Adam is a former teacher, assistant principal, principal, and director of innovation. He also travels the country giving keynotes, doing leadership consulting, and holding professional development workshops for teachers and leaders alike. Rae's students are right in front of her, and Adam's are scattered all around the country. Regardless of our titles, we are both educators—through and through. We know what it's like to be in the trenches.

We wrote this book because we live it, we see it, we breathe it, we talk it, we write it, we grapple with it, we podcast it, we commiserate with it, we laugh at it, and most of all we want it to improve, because teachers deserve it, all of it, every single day.

Thank you for reading—and don't stop fighting. Don't stop fighting for what you know is right. For what's best for you and the kids you work with. For what you deserve, to make you as successful as you possibly can be. For those tiny little moments you have with your students that you'll remember for the rest of your life—that's what we fight for.

Don't stop fighting.

ACKNOWLEDGMENTS

ADAM WELCOME ACKNOWLEDGES

- To my family: Stacy, Greta, and Tilden bring more joy to my life than anything else in the world.
- To my dad, who taught second grade for thirty plus years and was the epitome of an innovative, fun, caring, and balanced teacher.
- To teachers: to all the teachers I've had as a student, worked with as a colleague or facilitator, mentored, pushed, and laughed with over the years. Thank you for all that you've done, all you continue to do, and all of your future endeavors.

RAE HUGHART ACKNOWLEDGES

- To the Teach Better Team, for opening my eyes to the impact educators can make not only for their students but for one another.
- To Jim and Julie Ford and their relentless focus on working toward your passion and taking each moment as an opportunity for a connection.
- To Mike and Dana Hrymak, acting as the top cheerleaders from afar!
- To Sima Browne, my grandmother, for never allowing my learning disability to limit my success. Thank you for the years of after-school tutoring sessions and inspiration, which finally allowed me to achieve my dreams of going to college!
- To the friends who we always treated like family: Anne and Jeff Levin, Mary and Cary Johnson, Rabbi Paul and Cathy Cohen. Thank you for acting as second, third, and fourth parents.
- To my teaching team at EJHS for always cheering on the goofiness, embracing the weird, moving past the missteps, and celebrating the successes.

- To my former student Emma Bridgette for using her art skills to mock up cover designs for months on end when she heard about the possibility of a book dedicated to educators.
- To Mr. Harvey Dent and Mr. Alfred Pennyworth for more dog snuggles and love than a girl could ask for!

ABOUT THE AUTHORS

ADAM WELCOME is a best-selling author of the runaway favorite *Kids Deserve It* and the author of *Run Like a Pirate* and *Empower Our Girls*. He's a "20 To Watch" Technology Leader with the National School Board Association, and a former teacher, principal and director of innovation. A national speaker, he has an amazing wife and two children that keep life at home busy and so exciting. Adam is also an avid runner and has completed thirty marathons!

RAE HUGHART is a middle level math educator in Illinois, director of training and development for the Teach Better Team, and coauthor of the book *Teach Better*. Rae continues to facilitate rich discussions with educators around mastering personalized learning, providing targeted student-focused feedback, and the impact of incorporating purpose into daily learning. After being inducted into the Illinois State University Hall of Fame in 2017, Rae was awarded the 2018 First Place Henry Ford Teacher Innovator Award for her innovative educational impact.

INVITE THE AUTHORS TO YOUR NEXT EVENT

Adam has been a national speaker for the last five years and works with school districts all across the country. He has delivered hundreds of keynotes. Please contact him directly for more information on speaking.

adamwelcome@gmail.com

mradamwelcome.com

Rae has been supporting educators through keynotes and workshops for years. Working with school districts across the country, Rae's partnership with the Teach Better Team allows for opportunities for continual, personalized support. Please contact the team directly for more information on speaking.

Info@TeachBetter.com

TeachBetter.com

MORE FROM

Dave Burgess Consulting, Inc.

Since 2012, DBCI has been publishing books that inspire and equip educators to be their best. For more information on our titles or to purchase bulk orders for your school, district, or book study, visit **DaveBurgessconsulting.com/DBCIbooks**.

MORE INSPIRATION, PROFESSIONAL GROWTH & PERSONAL DEVELOPMENT

Be REAL by Tara Martin

Be the One for Kids by Ryan Sheehy

The Coach ADVenture by Amy Illingworth

Creatively Productive by Lisa Johnson

Educational Eye Exam by Alicia Ray

The EduNinja Mindset by Jennifer Burdis

Empower Our Girls by Lynmara Colón and Adam Welcome

Finding Lifelines by Andrew Grieve and Andrew Sharos

The Four O'Clock Faculty by Rich Czyz

How Much Water Do We Have? by Pete and Kris Nunweiler

If the Dance Floor is Empty, Change the Song by Dr. Joe Clark

P Is for Pirate by Dave and Shelley Burgess

A Passion for Kindness by Tamara Letter

The Path to Serendipity by Allyson Apsey

Sanctuaries by Dan Tricarico

The SECRET SAUCE by Rich Czyz

Shattering the Perfect Teacher Myth by Aaron Hogan

Stories from Webb by Todd Nesloney

Talk to Me by Kim Bearden

Teach Better by Chad Ostrowski, Tiffany Ott, Rae Hughart, and
 Jeff Gargas
Teach Me, Teacher by Jacob Chastain
Teach, Play, Learn! by Adam Peterson
TeamMakers by Laura Robb and Evan Robb
Through the Lens of Serendipity by Allyson Apsey
The Zen Teacher by Dan Tricarico

LIKE A PIRATE™ SERIES

Teach Like a PIRATE by Dave Burgess
eXPlore Like a Pirate by Michael Matera
Learn Like a Pirate by Paul Solarz
Play Like a Pirate by Quinn Rollins
Run Like a Pirate by Adam Welcome
Tech Like a PIRATE by Matt Miller

LEAD LIKE A PIRATE™ SERIES

Lead Like a PIRATE by Shelley Burgess and Beth Houf
Balance Like a Pirate by Jessica Cabeen, Jessica Johnson, and
 Sarah Johnson
Lead beyond Your Title by Nili Bartley
Lead with Appreciation by Amber Teamann and Melinda Miller
Lead with Culture by Jay Billy
Lead with Instructional Rounds by Vicki Wilson
Lead with Literacy by Mandy Ellis

LEADERSHIP & SCHOOL CULTURE

Culturize by Jimmy Casas
Escaping the School Leader's Dunk Tank by Rebecca Coda and
 Rick Jetter
From Teacher to Leader by Starr Sackstein
The Innovator's Mindset by George Couros

It's OK to Say "They" by Christy Whittlesey

Kids Deserve It! by Todd Nesloney and Adam Welcome

Live Your Excellence by Jimmy Casas

Let Them Speak by Rebecca Coda and Rick Jetter

The Limitless School by Abe Hege and Adam Dovico

Next-Level Teaching by Jonathan Alsheimer

The Pepper Effect by Sean Gaillard

The Principled Principal by Jeffrey Zoul and Anthony McConnell

Relentless by Hamish Brewer

The Secret Solution by Todd Whitaker, Sam Miller, and Ryan Donlan

Start. Right. Now. by Todd Whitaker, Jeffrey Zoul, and Jimmy Casas

Stop. Right. Now. by Jimmy Casas and Jeffrey Zoul

Teach Your Class Off by CJ Reynolds

They Call Me "Mr. De" by Frank DeAngelis

Unmapped Potential by Julie Hasson and Missy Lennard

Word Shift by Joy Kirr

Your School Rocks by Ryan McLane and Eric Lowe

TECHNOLOGY & TOOLS

50 Things You Can Do with Google Classroom by Alice Keeler
and Libbi Miller

50 Things to Go Further with Google Classroom by Alice Keeler
and Libbi Miller

140 Twitter Tips for Educators by Brad Currie, Billy Krakower,
and Scott Rocco

Block Breaker by Brian Aspinall

Code Breaker by Brian Aspinall

Control Alt Achieve by Eric Curts

Google Apps for Littles by Christine Pinto and Alice Keeler

Master the Media by Julie Smith

Reality Bytes by Christine Lion-Bailey, Jesse Lubinsky, and
Micah Shippee, PhD

Sail the 7 Cs with Microsoft Education by Becky Keene
and Kathi Kersznowski
Shake Up Learning by Kasey Bell
Social LEADia by Jennifer Casa-Todd
Stepping up to Google Classroom by Alice Keeler and
Kimberly Mattina
Teaching Math with Google Apps by Alice Keeler and
Diana Herrington
Teachingland by Amanda Fox and Mary Ellen Weeks

TEACHING METHODS & MATERIALS

All 4s and 5s by Andrew Sharos
Boredom Busters by Katie Powell
The Classroom Chef by John Stevens and Matt Vaudrey
The Collaborative Classroom by Trevor Muir
Copyrighteous by Diana Gill
Ditch That Homework by Matt Miller and Alice Keeler
Ditch That Textbook by Matt Miller
Don't Ditch That Tech by Matt Miller, Nate Ridgway, and
Angelia Ridgway
EDrenaline Rush by John Meehan
Educated by Design by Michael Cohen, The Tech Rabbi
The EduProtocol Field Guide by Marlena Hebern and Jon Corippo
The EduProtocol Field Guide: Book 2 by Marlena Hebern and
Jon Corippo
Instant Relevance by Denis Sheeran
LAUNCH by John Spencer and A. J. Juliani
Make Learning MAGICAL by Tisha Richmond
Pure Genius by Don Wettrick
The Revolution by Darren Ellwein and Derek McCoy
Shift This! by Joy Kirr
Skyrocket Your Teacher Coaching by Michael Cary Sonbert

Spark Learning by Ramsey Musallam

Sparks in the Dark by Travis Crowder and Todd Nesloney

Table Talk Math by John Stevens

The Wild Card by Hope and Wade King

The Writing on the Classroom Wall by Steve Wyborney

CHILDREN'S BOOKS

Beyond Us by Aaron Polansky

Cannonball In by Tara Martin

Dolphins in Trees by Aaron Polansky

I Want to Be a Lot by Ashley Savage

The Princes of Serendip by Allyson Apsey

The Wild Card Kids by Hope and Wade King

Zom-Be a Design Thinker by Amanda Fox

Made in the USA
Coppell, TX
19 November 2020